HOPE IN THE STRUGGLE

HOPE
IN THE
STRUGGLE

A Memoir

JOSIE R. JOHNSON

With Carolyn Holbrook and Arleta Little

University of Minnesota Press
Minneapolis
London

Published by the University of Minnesota Press
111 Third Avenue South, Suite 290
Minneapolis, MN 55401-2520
http://www.upress.umn.edu

Printed in the United States of America on acid-free paper

The University of Minnesota is an equal-opportunity educator and employer.

25 24 23 22 21 20 19   10 9 8 7 6 5 4 3 2 1

Library of Congress Cataloging-in-Publication Data
Johnson, Josie R., author. | with Carolyn Holbrook and Arleta Little
Hope in the struggle : a memoir / Josie R. Johnson ; with Arleta Little
    and Carolyn Holbrook.
Minneapolis, Minnesota : University of Minnesota Press, [2019] |
Identifiers: LCCN 2018046158 (print) | ISBN 978-1-5179-0444-9 (hc) |
    ISBN 978-1-5179-0445-6 (pb)
Subjects: LCSH: Johnson, Josie R. | African American women civil rights
workers—Biography. | Social justice—United States—History—20th century.
| African Americans—Civil rights—History—20th century. | African Ameri-
cans—Social conditions. | Civil rights workers—United States—Biography.
| African Americans—Minnesota—Minneapolis—Biography. | Minneapolis
(Minn.)—Biography. | BISAC: HISTORY / United States / State & Local /
Midwest (IA, IL, IN, KS, MI, MN, MO, ND, NE, OH, SD, WI).
Classification: LCC E185.97.J6925 A3 2019 (print) | DDC 323.092 [B] —dc23
LC record available at https://lccn.loc.gov/2018046158

For the ancestors who struggled for me

For the future generations for whom I struggle

Always in love and always for justice

Contents

Prologue

FOR MANY YEARS I have been asked to write a book. I never took the suggestion seriously or gave it much consideration—I was raised in a manner where the work I did for my community, for my people, was simply second nature. I saw this dedication in my parents, in my brothers; I see it now in my daughters and my granddaughters. I am one among many dedicated to fighting for justice and for our people. I am one among many who have been exposed to committed Black scholars, artists, activists, civil rights heroes, and survivors in the struggle for justice. I am not different from the others.

But, repeatedly, young Black people have asked me why I continue to work on issues of justice and how it is that I continue to have hope. I feel a responsibility to my biological and cultural family to answer these questions. In addition, many of my friends are no longer here, and our story must be told. With the understanding that each generation will find its own methods, these things challenge me now to find the words, to provide a context, to articulate a rationale for my years in the struggle.

My parents blessed me with childhood love and a sense of security. They raised me in a community where I felt protected. They talked with me and helped me learn who we were as a people. By teaching me to respect all people and to understand that in our struggle all contribute, they modeled for me how to love without hate. I inherited my values and my sense of duty and love for our people from my parents. These values have been a thorough and consistent guide in my life.

I believe that we carry the seeds of love and justice from our ancestors. I write this book for my children, grandchildren, and great-grandchildren with the hope that current and future generations will remember the strength of our ancestors, learn from my story, continue the struggle, and succeed in gaining justice for our people.

1

FAMILY VALUES

I OWE EVERYTHING to my parents and grandparents, to the community I grew up in. They all set fine examples for my two younger brothers and me in terms of family values, civic engagement, and pride in ourselves and our race. My parents, Judson Wilbur Robinson Sr. and Josie Bell McCullough Robinson, met in 1924 when they were students at Prairie View State Normal and Industrial College, a historically Black university in Prairie View, Texas (now Prairie View A&M University). Daddy wanted to go to law school but at that time there weren't any law schools that Blacks could attend in Texas or nearby states, so he took a degree in business instead, graduating in 1926. Mother graduated in 1929 with a degree in education. I was their firstborn child, arriving on October 7, 1930. My two brothers, Judson Jr. and Jim, were born two and four years later.

My parents were homeowners since the time of their marriage, right after my mother's graduation from college. Initially, they owned two homes: one in San Antonio near family, where I was born, and the other in Houston. During the Great Depression, many Black men worked on the railroad, and my father was a waiter on the Southern Pacific Railroad. We could not afford to keep two homes at the time, so Daddy decided Houston would be the best location

1

for us to live since the Southern Pacific operated from there. We moved when I was two years old, and my parents offered our San Antonio home to my maternal grandmother, Ida Irene Leonard, whom we kids called Mommie.

Mommie was a stately woman. She was stern yet kind and loving. Mommie taught my brothers and me, by word and example, that we could do anything in life that we wanted to do. Her first husband, my biological grandfather, Stuart McCullough, died when my mother was thirteen. Mommie later married a pharmacist, Dr. A. K. Leonard, and he was the one we called Grandpa since we never met Stuart. Mommie and Grandpa A.K. owned a drugstore in San Antonio, and Grandpa's brother William Henry owned another drugstore on the other side of town. Both stores served multiracial neighborhoods with mostly Black and Mexican families. Mommie and Grandpa's drugstore was known as Leonard's on the West Side and his brother's store was Leonard's on the East Side.

When I was about five years old, Grandpa A.K. was killed in a car accident while he and Mommie were on their way home from the funeral of his brother who lived in Corpus Christi. It was God's will that I wasn't in that tragic accident. My grandparents wanted me to ride back to San Antonio with them, but for some reason it was decided that I would ride with Mommie's best friend instead. If I had been in their car, it's likely that I too would have perished.

Mommie was seriously injured in the accident, but she recovered fully and resumed ownership and management of the drugstore. She was not a registered pharmacist, however, so she had to discontinue the pharmacy services. But Mommie was smart and tenacious, a good businesswoman and administrator. She continued providing her customers with full drugstore services except for prescriptions, selling non-pharmacy items and offering delivery and credit for people who needed those services. Like most drugstores at that time, there was a soda fountain in the store where customers could relax at tables and enjoy ice cream sodas and other beverages.

My brothers and I spent many Christmas holidays and summer vacations with Mommie, and I worked at Leonard's at the soda fountain making ice cream cones and floats. I also learned to roll cigarettes for customers who wanted to buy one or two at a time. Whenever customers called orders in on the phone, my brothers would deliver the orders on their bicycles. Mommie called my brothers and me official paid workers. "You are earning money for your school clothes," she would tell us. At the end of each day, I enjoyed helping with the bookkeeping and counting the day's receipts.

Mommie had high expectations of us. She fully expected my brothers to deliver orders quickly and efficiently, and for me to help manage the soda fountain and to know all of the items in the store in order to serve her customers fully. If a customer wanted something that I couldn't locate, I went to Mommie and she would show me where to find the item. "You must always do your work with honor and commitment," she told us, and that's how she worked. The store was open seven days a week from 8 a.m. until 8 p.m., except for Sundays when she opened later and one evening each week when she closed early. She used her business acumen to ensure that the store was well managed and to always let her customers know that she cared about them and valued their business.

Mommie owned and also lived in the same white frame building that housed her corner drugstore, and a heavy locked door separated her living quarters from the store. Her apartment included a large bedroom, a living room, her kitchen, bathroom, and a fenced-in yard with two red chow dogs that we walked around the neighborhood. She was very proud of us and was never short on praise for how well we did the jobs she assigned us and for serving the community. She had an extensive collection of dolls that she kept on her bed, all types of dolls: antique dolls, fashion dolls, dolls from many different parts of the world. I enjoyed spending time listening to her tell me stories about the history and culture of her dolls. She often invited her close friends to her home to see us and show them things we could do. I remember one time she asked me to sing her friends a song she thought I knew. I remember thinking, *Mommie, you know I don't carry a tune very well.* But at the end of the song she said I had sung it beautifully. This was one of so many ways that she and my parents encouraged me and built within me a sense of well-being and confidence in my abilities.

The neighborhood Mommie lived in was racially mixed, mostly African American and Mexican. Many of her customers were Mexican, but I don't think she spoke Spanish. She did, however, understand it well enough to be able to serve her Mexican customers. My best friend in San Antonio was a Mexican girl who lived across the street from Mommie, and we spent lots of time together biking, talking, and playing at each other's homes. I remember vividly that she did not want me to learn Spanish. "I don't want anyone to think you're Mexican," she would say but would not explain why. I thought that was so strange since we were friends. Her family moved away when the girl and I were about thirteen and I never saw her again.

There were lots of churches in our neighborhood, and my family was interdenominational—Daddy was African Methodist Episcopal (AME) and my paternal grandfather was a Baptist preacher. Mommie was also Baptist, but her two children, my mother and my Uncle Jim, later converted to Catholicism. I don't know why they converted. Back then, and in fact until Vatican II in 1962, Catholic teaching did not allow us to visit other churches. But my mother did not impose that restriction on us growing up. We usually didn't attend formal Sunday services in other churches because we went to Mass in our own church on Sundays. But we did visit those other churches with our friends, including the Church of God in Christ where we heard spirited gospel music and people shouting.

There was a Catholic cathedral a couple of blocks from the drugstore where we went to Mass when we visited Mommie. My mother felt strongly about going to Mass on Sundays. Even though my father attended AME services, he also often reminded us, "If you are too ill to go to Mass, I guess you are too ill to do anything else that day." One Sunday morning when I was in my early teens I fainted in church. We had gone to Mass after having arrived in San Antonio very late that Saturday night. When Mass had ended and I got up from the pew to go outside, the next thing I knew I was surrounded by Mexican women who had revived me. They were all speaking Spanish and I didn't understand a word they were saying. I will never forget the smiles on their faces or the love in their voices and their eyes when they saw that I was okay. That experience taught me the universality of love.

During the school year, we lived in Houston. Our first home there was on the northern end of the Second Ward. The ward system had been a common political tool in the early nineteenth century, and Houston's civic leaders had divided the city into four initial wards in 1839. The Fifth Ward was added in 1866 to accommodate the city's growth, and the Sixth Ward was added around a decade later. The city's form of government changed in 1906, but the wards have remained a cultural touchstone, especially in the areas that have remained primarily Black residential areas—the Second, Third, and Fifth Wards. The wards disappeared from Houston's city maps altogether in 1928, but area residents still identify certain communities as wards, with ward identification appearing on signage and in casual conversation between Houstonians. Today, they are cultural rather than legal identities.

6

Our house on Rusk Street was built high off the ground, and there was a space underneath the front porch where my brothers and I and our friends would hide and play. Inside the house were our bedrooms, living and dining rooms, and the bathroom. Our parents' bedroom had a large picture window that looked out onto the porch. The house was near the homes of Mommie's two sisters, my great aunts, Josie and Ninny Sasser—my mother was named after her Aunt Josie and I was named for my mother. I continued the tradition by naming my youngest daughter Josie, and then my middle daughter, Norrene, named her daughter Josie. So far there are five Josies through five generations of my family.

The northern end of the Second Ward was an industrial area with warehouses and railroad tracks. Both of my great aunts owned rooming houses there for white workers in the area. Mommie and her sisters were very light-skinned. One could surmise that Aunt Josie and Aunt Ninny were passing for white, because in the segregated South, Black men did not drive trucks or operate trains. Visiting my great aunts, which we didn't do often, was quite a treat; when we visited we had to enter their homes through the back door and stay in the kitchen. The only reason we were given was that the front door was for the renters. Aunt Josie was my mother's favorite aunt, and I have fond memories of our visits with her. The best thing about our visits was that Aunt Josie had a sugar sifter—a large jar that was placed on a stand and was filled with sugar. There was a lid on the bottom of the jar with a handle, and when you turned the handle, the sugar would sift out. We loved to spread butter on bread and then sprinkle sugar on top. It was delicious.

One day when Aunt Josie didn't have any renters, she let me see the house. I was impressed with how lovely her home was. The rooms on the first floor were large and filled with antique furniture, including a beautiful white baby grand piano in the living room. The bedrooms on the second floor were as beautifully furnished as the rooms on the first floor.

There was also a corner store on our side of Rusk Street where we children could buy candy and gum. The store was owned by a person with light skin, possibly white. Except for the owner of the corner store, we were a small, Black, close-knit community. Everyone looked after the children on the block, and we could be chastised by any of the adults or reminded to behave.

There were railroad tracks on the next street over from our house on Rusk. The homes on that block were shotgun-style houses, houses made of cheap materials and designed so poorly that if you looked through the front door you could peer all the way to the back door with no obstruction, seeing the bedroom, kitchen, and bathroom on either side of the hall. We knew all the families on that street, but we knew the Mills family better than the others. One night a train caused a terrible fire in the Mills family's home. My parents invited them to stay with us until they could figure out what to do. Their daughter Ola, who was my age, lived with us for several years and became like a sister to me.

One of my deep memories from our Rusk Street home was the night my brother Judson Jr. took very sick and had a seizure. I must have been about five years old. He was two years younger than I so he must have been about three. I clearly remember how frightened my poor mother was. Somehow, word got out and our home was soon filled with neighbor ladies who took charge. A couple of the stronger women brought a galvanized tub into the middle room, our living/dining room, and filled it with water. The women placed my little brother in the water and, true to an old wives' tale from that time, they placed a spoon handle in his mouth to prevent him from swallowing his tongue. It seems that the water treatment was very important because they kept bathing him until the seizure stopped. I remember standing in the corner crying and praying silently that my little brother wouldn't die as I watched my mother—oh, how she cried and cried. Thankfully, he recovered. My father wasn't home that night. In those days, for his railroad work, he was away two or three times a week.

I have fond memories of going to the depot to pick up my father after his shift. His train usually came in at night, so Mom would dress us in our pajamas and pile us into our old dark gray Lincoln and off we'd go. At the station, we'd sit in the car and listen. Eyes lighting up, we would squeal, "Daddy's coming!" when we heard the rumble of the train pulling up to the station, accompanied by the mournful sound of its whistle. We waited as patiently as children wait for anything while we watched people leave the station, passengers first and then the workers. The porters and waiters were always the last to get off. We were so delighted when we finally spotted our tall, handsome father. "Hi children," he would say, greeting us with hugs. Then he would climb into the driver's seat and kiss Mother as she moved over to the passenger seat. "Daddy, will you take us to Galveston?" one of us would always ask. Daddy knew we would be asleep before we got home, but in his wisdom he also knew we would be very disappointed if he said no. We loved going to Galveston. It was a recreation city, and when we went there we had so much fun playing in the Gulf of Mexico, building sandcastles, collecting rocks, and going to the hot-dog stand. But Galveston was fifty-six miles from Houston and in those days, long before freeways were built, fifty-six miles was a long way away, so we didn't go very often. "Sure," he would respond, laughing as he drove away from the curb to take us home. "We're off to Galveston."

I will never forget the time one evening when we were on our way to pick up Daddy. It was dusk but still light enough outside to see. We were stopped for some reason, and I remember looking up and seeing a Black man crossing the street. He stepped aside and tipped his hat in deference to the white people he encountered while crossing the street. His demeanor changed once he got to the other side of the street, and we could hear him using language that showed his true feelings about having to accommodate white supremacy while crossing that street. I remember being so struck by seeing that even as a child.

When I was five or six years old, we moved out of our house on Rusk Street to a home on the corner of Nagle and McIlhanney Streets in the Third Ward. That house was much larger than our home on Rusk: we had a screened-in porch, a garage, a backyard that was surrounded by a picket fence, and each of us kids had our own room. We did our laundry on the porch where our washing machine sat with tubs for rinsing beside it. A side door led from the screened-in porch to the outside. I remember that the city had to put drains in the streets because of flooding that occurred when it rained, and how I crawled through the pipes with my brothers on days when it wasn't raining. I could do anything they could do even though I was the only girl. One day they blocked the ends of the pipe and I couldn't get out. They only kept me in there long enough to scare me, and indeed I was frightened and very angry with them.

I was nine years old when World War II started, several years after we moved to Nagle Street. The government encouraged citizens all across the country to plant victory gardens to help prevent a food shortage. It was also announced that DuPont's nylon manufacturing would be used exclusively to produce war materials. DuPont ceased production of nylon stockings and switched to parachutes, airplane cords, and ropes, and women were asked to save used nylons. Tobacco was also rationed and citizens were encouraged to save the metallic material inside cigarette packs.

Certain foods were rationed, and the planting of victory gardens helped ensure that there would be enough food for soldiers fighting around the world. The gardens also helped people stretch their ration coupons, provided by the government to limit the amount of certain items that people could have. Being a civic-minded man, my father saw the importance of participating in this effort. He also saw it as an opportunity to teach me gardening as an act of civic engagement. We grew lettuce, mustard and collard greens, tomatoes. I remember going out to the garden every morning with Daddy with watering cans, picking ripe vegetables for Mother to cook.

At dinnertime our family was proud to eat the vegetables Daddy and I grew in our victory garden. We always ate breakfast and dinner together, even when Daddy was away on a railroad trip. Dinner always began with grace being said, and every day our parents asked how our day had been and listened carefully as each of us answered. Mother always cooked more than enough food and often there were neighbors or Daddy's colleagues at our dinner table. My parents were avid followers of the accomplishments of Black people, and dinner conversations were always lively and informative, whether we had company or not. For instance, though I was only six years old when Jesse Owens won the Olympics, I remember Mom and Daddy discussing his victory and white people's negative reaction to it.

I don't remember a time when my parents didn't instill in my brothers and me the importance of civic engagement. Throughout my childhood, Daddy organized and served on multiple boards and committees, including the NAACP. He also helped organize the first Urban League affiliate in Houston and was president of the Railroad Waiters Union.

My mother was what is known today as a stay-at-home mom, but she too served the community. When we were young, she acted as a sort of community social worker, advising and helping out whoever needed help. She earned extra income teaching uneducated, middle-class white women to read and write. I clearly remember going with her to those women's back doors and sitting with her in their kitchens while she gave them their lessons. Later, when Jim, Judson Jr., and I were in high school, she volunteered to teach African American history at the segregated Black Catholic school we attended. She put her education degree to full use after we were in college and was an early pioneer in the concept of early childhood education. She created a nursery school that became a model for educating small children: she not only listened to the children and talked with them but also cared for their young minds, teaching them reading, writing, and arithmetic. Her school became a practicum placement for education majors at Texas Southern University. I remember feeling so proud of her whenever I visited her school when I was home from college for holidays and summer vacation. I simply couldn't get enough of watching how completely and naturally she engaged students who wanted to learn how to teach children who were so young.

Mother made our home the center of our community. I remember her calling out to our neighbors on her way out of the garage, "Hey, Miss So-and-so, I'm going to the store. Do you need anything?" For a short while, she raised chickens in the backyard of our house on Nagle Street. Rather than confining them to a coop, she converted a small space in the yard so that the chicks could roam free. When they grew to broiler size she sold them. This only lasted a year or so because Mother felt badly about growing the chickens only to sell them, knowing they would become someone's meal.

My mother was an incredibly energetic woman, which is remarkable because she suffered rheumatic fever as a child that damaged her heart. She may not have had as much strength as she appeared to have, but she never let it stop her. I can remember her feeling very ill at the end of some days. She wasn't herself at those times—her energy was subdued, as though it was being drained from her. We were so worried when we saw her like that and feared she was going to die. In those days, doctors prescribed digitalis to heart patients.

Mother would place the small pill under her tongue and go straight to bed. Following an episode she would begin her next day an hour later but would soon be back to her routine. I never saw her spend an entire day in bed.

Mother and Aunt Josie were very close. When Mother wasn't feeling well, Aunt Josie would tell us that we must take care of her. When Aunt Josie herself became ill and was no longer as independent as she had once been, Mother, concerned that she may not eat as well as she should, took her nutritious home-cooked meals nearly every day.

My brothers and I went to St. Nicholas, a historically Black Catholic school in the Third Ward managed by nuns from the Sisters of the Holy Family, an order of African American nuns founded by free Black women in New Orleans in 1842—twenty years before the Civil War and before it was legal for such a congregation to exist. Education was the assignment of the Houston branch of the Sisters of the Holy Family, and indeed we received a high-quality education. Our principal, Sister Anselm, and the nuns she managed were strict, insisting that we be orderly and treat one another and our school building with respect.

Our home was near Jack Yates High School, a large public Black high school that had sports, shop, and other subjects that our small Catholic school did not have. After I graduated, my brothers transferred to Jack Yates, though I'm not sure why my parents waited until I graduated to allow my brothers to attend that school.

The city parks were segregated, but we knew that the swimming pools in the white parks were deeper and better serviced than the pool in Emancipation Park, the Black park, allowing white kids to dive if they wanted to. My brothers were good swimmers but were limited by the shallowness of our pool. Our playground equipment was also notably inferior to the equipment in the white park. Black families were invited to visit the white parks on special days such as Juneteenth, the day celebrated every June to commemorate the signing of the Emancipation Proclamation. We did not attend. Our parents believed adamantly that we would not honor the days that whites said we should honor. I remember them saying, "If you can't go to their park every day, you can't go on special days either."

We often went to visit my paternal grandparents, Henry and Willie Robinson, who lived nearby. Grandma Willie had long white hair and I enjoyed brushing and braiding it. Grandpa Henry had only finished eighth grade, but he somehow managed to go to "college." Back in the 1800s, when he attended Huston-Tillotson in Austin, the school only went through eighth grade. Later it became Huston-Tillotson University, a historically Black university. Whenever Daddy or his sister, my Aunt Verona, wrote letters to their father, he would return them marked all over with corrections in red ink. He wanted to be sure his children could read well, write legibly, and use proper English in their writing as well as their speaking.

Grandpa Henry was a preacher. My brothers and I were told stories of Grandma Willie standing in the back of their Baptist church watching and listening while Grandpa Henry preached his sermons. If she heard anyone in the congregation say anything negative about him, she quickly corrected them. Grandpa was what we called a "travelin' preacha." He traveled to many communities near Houston teaching Black preachers the Bible and effective preaching methods.

When I was in my teens, we took frequent road trips from Houston to San Antonio to visit Mommie in Daddy's old Lincoln. We noticed water fountains and restrooms with signs that read "White Only" or "Colored Only." There were even rest areas on the road that were designated as "Negro areas." San Antonio is 197 miles from Houston; in those days the speed limit was forty-five miles per hour, so the trip took about five hours. Mother packed food to take on those trips, and we stopped at the homes of friends along the way to rest and use the bathroom. Though our parents taught us much about racism and taught us pride in who we were, directly experiencing the things that we had been told about brought them to life for us. Daddy tried to ease our concerns by making up stories or telling jokes about why we couldn't stop. I don't remember his words, just a feeling of joy as he told his stories.

Daddy was a real pioneer and trendsetter. In 1943, when I was thirteen, he became the first African American to manage Kelly Courts, a public housing project in the Fifth Ward. The following year he took me with him as he went knocking on doors in our neighborhood and in the projects to fight for voters' rights. I remember us going door-to-door collecting signatures to do away with the oppressive Poll Tax, a tax implemented throughout the South to prevent Blacks from voting.

Three years later, he was promoted to manager of the Cuney Homes project located in the Third Ward. He also became the first Black realtor in Houston and the first Black man to own an insurance agency there. He had many friends and supporters for all of his endeavors, both political and business, and I remember that white men in his business called him Mr. Robinson. They never called him by his first name unless he gave them permission to do so. Mother was perhaps his strongest supporter and cheerleader. She encouraged everything he wanted to do, somehow finding financial support for all of his efforts. Initially, he managed his business out of our home, and I was his first secretary. He had a map of Houston that hung on the dining room wall. I will never forget the day he got his first pair of reading glasses. He walked up to the map, put on the round, metal rimmed spectacles, and a big smile spread over his face. "I can see!" he exclaimed.

It was my family that started me on the lifelong path of fighting for social justice, and they strongly supported my efforts, but there were other things that helped solidify my path. Growing up, my best friend was a girl named Joyce Mouton. We had so much fun together—we walked to school together and often dressed alike. Her mother worked weekends, so Joyce essentially became part of our family and, in fact, became my eldest daughter Patrice's godmother. We are still the best of friends.

When I was in high school, Joyce experienced a crushing emotional trauma that affected her so deeply that she still feels it today. Her strongest, and perhaps only, desire growing up was to join the convent upon graduating high school and become a nun. We both worked hard to do everything right so that I could go to college and Joyce could enter the convent.

By the time of our graduation, I had been accepted to Fisk University and Joyce was eagerly looking forward to joining the convent. But a week before graduation, she received a letter telling her that she had not been accepted. Her biological father and mother were not together. Her mother and stepfather had tried to get the marriage to Joyce's biological father annulled, but the church refused them, saying that they did not view her biological father as a Christian. They used this to deny Joyce entry into the convent. It was a horrible blow. Friends and family had selected all of her graduation gifts with the convent in mind, and she had to give them to someone else who was accepted to the convent.

Many years later, one of our deacons at church went to a class on annulment and learned that there was a form Blacks were required to fill out in order to be granted annulment. No one had told Joyce's parents about this form; even worse, the deacon learned that whites were not required to take this step. It was horribly shocking to learn that even in the church discrimination existed. We were keenly aware of the unjust gender discrimination in the church; priests were allowed to walk through society without their collars on, but nuns had to wear their habits at all times and were not allowed to ride buses unless accompanied by a chaperone, usually a parishioner. Further, priests were allowed to take meals wherever and with whomever they wished but nuns were not. I remember thinking, "This is so unfair." Like nuns everywhere, the nuns at St. Nicholas took vows of poverty, charity, and obedience. But true to her activism and community spirit, Mother often invited them to our home for meals. Honoring their vow of privacy, she allowed them to take their meals in our breakfast nook with the door closed. But it wasn't until the deacon attended this class that we learned of the laws that existed within the church that permitted such blatant racial discrimination.

This was especially shocking because we learned that the Catholic Church had their own racist rules. We remained loyal to the church, but looking back I often wonder that my reaction was so strong. As such a young person, I didn't know how to bring justice to that situation, but I attribute my awareness to things I had learned at home; for instance, I knew of the work of Thurgood Marshall and Adam Clayton Powell. What happened to Joyce brought my awareness of the discrimination that was happening in my own life to the surface. Joyce was the smartest girl in our class. Her mother was a consistent volunteer at school and in our church. But at the time, because her rejection was blamed on her biological father, Joyce wondered if there was something essentially wrong with her. She wasn't able to see back then that it was not about her at all. It was all about discrimination.

Today Joyce is able to see that there was a blessing in her inability to attend the convent. She graduated from Xavier University, the only university in the United States that is both Catholic and a historically Black university, and she taught religion courses in her parish until her retirement. She married a wonderful man, and they have five children who now are all nearing retirement. Whereas Joyce was denied the opportunity to be a nun, the love and commitment to service that she carried with her could not be denied. The discrimination she suffered did not destroy her.

I too worried over Joyce's experience in the church and the hurt that she felt in being denied her dream. I didn't fully understand at the time the connection between her denial and racism. When I later learned it was a matter of the church not sharing important information with Joyce, my feelings toward the church and its role in supremacy became an important issue. I needed to begin paying closer attention to the universality of supremacy, even in my own church.

Even as I grieved Joyce's predicament, I was still excited to start preparing for college life. I initially wanted to go to Howard, but Mother thought it was too far away from home. She wanted me to go to Fisk: being in Nashville it was closer to home, and a lot of Fisk people lived in Houston and were very much engaged in the community. Happily for us both, I was accepted to Fisk. That summer before leaving for college my friend Edwina's mother, Mrs. Gray, took me, Edwina, and another friend, Anita Jemison, under her wing to prepare us for life at Fisk. "Fisk students represent their families, the university, and indeed our community both on and off campus," she reminded us. She met with us regularly for several weeks and taught us grooming and etiquette. I think of it today as her own private finishing school for emerging Fiskites. At the end of summer—and at the end of Mrs. Gray's teaching—I was off to Nashville.

2

FISK UNIVERSITY—
RACIAL PRIDE
AND SOCIAL UPLIFT

FROM THE DAY the decision was made that I would attend Fisk University it was all I could think about. Going to Fisk meant everything to me. I remember telling our family doctor of my interest in serving my community by becoming a nurse and maybe someday a doctor. He encouraged me to go directly into major studies that would make me eligible for admission to medical school. Dr. Miner was a tall, kind, jovial man who did his undergraduate studies at Fisk and then went on to medical school at Meharry Medical College, located across the street from Fisk. He frequently told me, "You need to go to Fisk so you can prepare to go to Meharry. I want you to take over my practice when I retire." My family and I took Dr. Miner's advice very seriously. When the day finally arrived when I would leave home for college, a hot August day in 1947, I waved good-bye to Mother, Daddy, and my brothers as the train chugged away from the Houston depot. "Be very careful," Mother mouthed. I was sixteen years old and very excited to be on my way to Fisk with the intention of studying medicine.

Trains in the South were segregated back then. The white passengers who rode first class sat in comfortable cars with plush seating and picture windows covered with blinds and curtains and small tables serviced by Black waiters dressed in sparkling white jackets and aprons, bow ties at their necks, and who kept their glasses full and plates laden with snacks. White passengers who rode in coach also had windows. Black passengers were relegated to small, crowded sections in the back of train cars with no access to waiters, porters, or the dining cars.

Thirteen years before I left for Fisk, when Daddy worked as a dining car waiter on the Southern Pacific Railroad, he had organized the Dining Car Waiters Union and served as its first president. He maintained the friendship and respect of the men who were still working on the railroad even though he had left to start his own business when I was still in high school. Knowing that I would be alone on the train for some six hours, Daddy had contacted railroad friends and asked them to look out for me. It was hot on the train, but Daddy's friends made the long ride more enjoyable by bringing me an occasional sandwich or a cool drink, always with a smile and a "Howdy do, young lady," along with congratulations on my accomplishment and words of encouragement. Their faces beamed along with mine when they told me what a great man my father was.

My parents fully expected that my brothers and I would go to college. And many of my parents' friends were Fisk alums: doctors, attorneys, teachers, and others who worked in professions that provided excellent service to our community. The way Dr. Miner and our family friends described their experiences at Fisk made me very excited to be on my way there. "The scholarship is excellent," they often explained, telling us about their exceptional professors and the classes they had taken. And they spoke of distinguished alumni who had returned as speakers: W. E. B. Du Bois; Ida B. Wells; Mahala Dickerson, the first Black president of the National Association of Women Lawyers; Alfred O. Coffin, the first African American to earn a Ph.D. in zoology; and many others.

When I arrived in Nashville, I was greeted by a group of

three or four smiling students who had driven to the depot in a truck to welcome me. Arriving at Fisk, the driver removed my trunk and placed it in the basement of Jubilee Hall. The group then led me through the basement and into the foyer, and I remember thinking that I must really be excited about being at Fisk to have been so happy just to walk through a basement.

When we reached the foyer, my student escorts allowed me a few moments to take in the beauty. I was awestruck at the sight of the beautiful and historic women's dormitory. It was a massive Victorian Gothic structure that featured a towering steeple and magnificent doors. If you walked through the front door, you immediately saw the tastefully decorated foyer with lovely, comfortable places for residents and their guests to sit and talk. A well-dressed receptionist sat behind an elegant desk and to the right of the desk was the most exquisite, gracious staircase I had ever seen. Wide at the bottom and secured by matching pillars and dark wooden banisters on either side, the uncarpeted staircase was adorned by balusters in alternating dark and light wood that had been sent from Sierra Leone, West Africa, by a former student. Large rooms were on either side of the foyer, tastefully decorated in blue and gold—Fisk's colors—and in one of those rooms was a finely tuned, elegant baby grand piano.

Jubilee Hall is the most striking of Fisk's buildings and perhaps the most famous college residence hall in the world. It was constructed with proceeds from the university's Jubilee Singers' historic 1871–74 international tour. Fisk was facing extreme financial difficulties at the time, so the Jubilee Singers, an a cappella group whose name derives from a biblical reference to the Year of the Jubilee in the book of Leviticus, went on an eighteen-month tour, performing in Pennsylvania, Ohio, New York, Connecticut, Rhode Island, New Jersey, Massachusetts, Maryland, and Washington, D.C. They also traveled to London, where they performed for the Duke and Duchess of Argyll and for Queen Victoria. The tour was grueling due to racism, neglect, hunger, and harsh weather, but in the end they raised $40,000, which was a lot of money in those days and enough to keep their beloved school open. And in the process, they raised awareness of Negro spirituals in states beyond the South and in England.

The male student who had taken responsibility for my large traveling trunk had carefully placed it on the floor in the basement, and when the girls knew I was ready, they began helping me unpack. In the era that I went to college, most people traveled by train, and many packed wardrobe travel trunks if they were going someplace where they would be staying for a while. The trunks were equipped with four to six drawers on one side and a rack with hangers on the other side. Each of us took a drawer from my trunk or a handful of clothes on hangers and began the trek up to the fourth floor where freshman women were housed. On the way up the stairs, I could hear the receptionist announcing phone calls over a loudspeaker for residents who would then make their way to the phone that was mounted on the wall in the middle of each floor. If the receptionist announced a visitor, the resident, always appropriately dressed, would rush down to the foyer to meet her guests.

When we finally made it to the fourth floor and the girls led me to my room, I was a little surprised to see how small the rooms were—attic-style rooms with slanted ceilings and limited closet space. Three freshman women were assigned to share each of the rooms. I remember that one of my room-mates was a bit messy. There was one chair in our room and she always piled her clothes on it.

My surprise was soon replaced by excitement when freshman week activities began; tours of the campus, intro-ductions to faculty and staff, placement exams, lectures and other academic activities during the day. Every night after we were finished with the hard work of the day, there were meet-and-greet gatherings on the Oval, the campus yard. Music students and those trying out for the Jubilee Singers serenaded us. The piano students then drew us to the elegant Jubilee Hall foyer where we sang and laughed together. It was such fun bonding with my freshman peers. I also learned that week that the manners and good grooming that Mrs. Gray had taught us would come in very handy, because along with the academic activities and the fun gatherings, we were expected to exhibit proper dress and good manners at all times. As Mrs. Gray had emphasized, a Fisk student represents her Black community, on campus and off.

World War II had ended two years before I went to college, so there were a lot of veterans enrolled at Fisk. They were very aware of the racial discrimination in our nation even for them, though they had served our country by fighting in the war. The bigotry we faced when we went into downtown Nashville was intense. Whites accepted everyone except Black people. It didn't make any difference that as Fisk students we were better educated and more well-dressed than many of the whites who refused to serve us.

Our theater department noted that the only way we were able to get items that we needed for campus plays such as costumes, props, and other equipment was to send the fair-skinned students to town because they would be seen as white. Some of the ways the white people showed their disdain were so ridiculous that we enjoyed playing games with them. Sometimes, just for fun our male students would dress in dashikis and speak Pig Latin when they went into town. Bus drivers, store clerks, and restaurant personnel thought they were African and served them. Even in the face of hatred, we were finding creative ways to beat the system.

In addition to my regular liberal arts courses, I was placed in a high mathematics group my first year. I didn't believe I belonged in that group and told my father that I planned to drop the class. "You hang in there and do your best," he said and calmly reminded me that I had to keep the tradition of our family and our people. "We do not quit," he said.

As my family's friends had told me, we Fisk students were fortunate to have excellent faculty. Harlem Renaissance poet, novelist, and librarian Arna Bontemps was our head librarian, expanding what was then the world's largest collection of African American cultural items. The great Harlem Renaissance modernist and avant-garde artist Aaron Douglas taught art classes. Dr. Inez Adams was associate professor of sociology and anthropology, and Evelyn Banks taught mathematics. Saint Elmo Brady, one of the first African Americans to achieve eminence in chemistry, was my chemistry professor and mentor, and Gladys Ford, from Houston, was my English and theater professor. Perhaps one of the most exciting things to happen while I was at Fisk was that in my freshman year the Board of Trustees appointed the noted social scientist Charles Spurgeon Johnson to become Fisk's first Black president.

We spent many an afternoon vigorously debating issues of race during afternoon gatherings in the Quaker house. The Quakers have a history of engaging in issues of justice, fairness, and education. Representatives of the Quaker faith were on Fisk's staff, and they supported our education without question. Throughout my years at Fisk, every phase of our experience from Africa to slavery to emancipation and beyond was discussed frequently, and national personalities often appeared on our campus to discuss strategies for freedom. We were exposed to many of the great Black intellectuals, scholars, musicians, historians, writers, activists, and critical thinkers of the time: Supreme Court Justice Thurgood Marshall, sociologist and historian W.E.B. Du Bois, civil rights activist Roy Wilkins, just to name a few. They not only lectured but offered us wonderful opportunities to engage in quality conversations with them. In addition, every religious thought was respected and discussed at Fisk. Every Friday evening, students gathered in the campus chapel while a music professor played soft music on the piano or organ. We had the option of simply sitting and thinking or, if we wished, we could go to the pulpit and express our thoughts and feelings. I truly enjoyed that weekly experience. It gave me such a wonderful feeling of peace, relaxation, and reflection at the end of the week.

I was very active in student activities during my four years at Fisk. I was president of the Newman Club (Fisk's Catholic student organization), served on the Dormitory Council and the Women's Senate, and was a member of the Tanner Art Club. I served on the Sociology Club's executive committee in my sophomore, junior, and senior years, and on the executive committee of the Stage Crafters Club in my junior year. I joined the Booster Club my sophomore year and was named Miss Booster in my junior year. I served as a summer retreater, welcoming new students to our campus during my junior year and was a Junior Counselor that same year. I was Attendant to the Alpha Sweetheart in my freshman year and was Attendant to the Omega Sweetheart in my junior year. I served on the staff of our yearbook, *The Oval,* in my junior and senior years. I was voted Queen of my freshman class and was Queen of the Music Festival in my junior year. I was inducted into Delta Sigma Theta sorority my junior year and was also voted Miss Fisk that year.

My social life was also very active. I had a wonderful group of friends who spent much time together talking and laughing and taking long walks on weekends. I dated a young man from San Antonio named Harold Jones during my sophomore year. I remember that Mommie did not like him—I don't think I ever knew why. During World War II and immediately after the war, the armed services offered full four-year scholarships to students who volunteered to serve for two years. When I told Mommie that Harold had accepted the offer and joined the army, she was relieved.

Before he left, Harold asked his close friends to protect his "interests" (meaning me). It seemed like I couldn't turn around without one of his friends checking on me or watching me. One Sunday afternoon while my friends and I were walking in the park enjoying the beauty of the landscape, listening to the songs of the birds and discussing politics and Black history as we did every weekend, I found myself deeply engaged in a conversation with Charles "Chuck" Johnson, an engineering student who was also from San Antonio. He had been a part of the group all along, but we hadn't paid much attention to each other until that day. I found him incredibly interesting—his intellect was outstanding. I soon began to look forward to our weekly walks in the park so that we could talk more. We talked about many, many things that were meaningful to both of us, and over time we discovered that we shared many values. We started dating in our junior year.

My life's direction took a change near the end of my college years. Having grown up in an environment of service to the community, I had gone to Fisk with intentions of going to medical school. Dr. Miner, our family doctor, was serving the community when he made house calls to the sick. During those visits, we always talked about our community and its needs. Looking back, I believe my interest in medicine came from wanting both to address my mother's illness and to do the things Dr. Miner talked about: service to community through medicine. And indeed my studies from my freshman year until the middle of my junior year reflected that plan. But over time, certain things I heard from medical students about unpleasant, even scary things they saw or had to do as assignments made me fearful, and I began to lose interest in completing my plan.

My roommate, Beatrice Jourdain, was a sociology major. She often talked about her courses, her research, and the exciting fieldwork she was doing with poor Black families and children in segregated Nashville and around the state of Tennessee. She shared with me the research of Fisk's President Johnson, and we had long conversations about the condition of our people and the difference she believed she could make through her studies. When she was assigned a research project that utilized a very new method, using punch cards to record key responses of her research subjects, she received permission for me to go with her to a few of her interviews. That was when I fully understood her excitement about her studies.

The more Bea talked about her field, coupled with what I saw for myself when I accompanied her, the more interested I became in sociology. It was so much more people-oriented than my chemistry major. Besides, my male friends who were medical students constantly drilled into me that "being a doctor is very hard for a woman," which at the time only reinforced my fear that I probably wouldn't make it through medical school. I wanted to change my major but my promise to Dr. Miner made such a decision very difficult. He was anticipating that I would take over his practice when he retired, and I wanted to keep my word. But I couldn't ignore my growing excitement about the field of sociology. I knew it was my true calling.

Thanks to a wise adviser and the support of my family, I was able to change my major from chemistry to the far more satisfying field of sociology. Through hard work and support, I was able to graduate on time with a sociology major and a chemistry minor. My adviser and the school admissions director told me that this major/minor combination would probably never happen again. To the best of my knowledge, it has not. Later, I began to realize that my decision to change my major may well have been unconsciously influenced by my mother's community work: her teaching, volunteering, and "feeding the community," as she always said.

My intention was to go right into graduate studies in sociology. However, while my father was in Nashville for my graduation, Chuck Johnson asked for my hand in marriage. He had received a Rockefeller scholarship to Massachusetts Institute of Technology (MIT) and wanted me to accompany him to Boston as his wife. My father agreed, and Chuck and I became engaged and planned to marry shortly after graduation.

Looking back on my years at Fisk University, I realize that it was there that I was able to begin actualizing all that I had been exposed to in my life, and where learning and new ideas could be tested and expanded on. It is where I learned the scholarship that supported what I had witnessed growing up in a home and community that taught me the value that our ancestors place on education and service through examples of parental teachings, community work, and the way the people around me lived. My experiences at Fisk, coupled with the values my parents instilled in me, helped create a tireless desire to be deeply involved with the struggle of my people.

3

A GROWING FAMILY,
A WIDER WORLD

CHUCK AND I WERE MARRIED before a small group of family and friends on June 27, 1951. Chuck wasn't Catholic, so he had to take marriage preparation counseling to learn how marriage is viewed in the Catholic Church. He had to promise that our children would be baptized and raised in the Catholic tradition. This was before the Second Vatican Council, in 1957, which among other things made it possible for Catholics to pray with other Christian denominations and encouraged friendship with other non-Christian faiths. We were not allowed to be married inside the Church, so with permission our wedding ceremony was officiated by a priest in front of the Blessed Mother's Grotto at my home parish, St. Nicholas Catholic Church. We wanted our family and friends to celebrate with us, so we held our wedding reception at my parents' home in Pleasantville, a new subdivision and housing development on the outskirts of Houston that my father and his partners had developed while I was in college. The community had public and private housing opportunities; my parents bought a home in the private housing section, and my mother managed the public housing section. Their new home was perfect for our reception.

We decided to spend our first summer as a married couple with Chuck's parents in San Antonio, taking occasional trips to Houston to visit my family. Later that summer we would head to Boston, where Chuck would be very busy pursuing a Ph.D. in engineering and mathematics at MIT. When would we have another opportunity to see our families?

Chuck's parents were kind and caring. Like my dad, Chuck's father, Miles T. Johnson (known as M.T. by his family and friends), had been a railroad man. M.T. was a solidly built, dark-skinned man who was meticulous and methodical and rather reserved in personality. Though long retired when we married, M.T. still worked every day. He got up at the same time each morning and came to the breakfast table neatly dressed in well-pressed pants and a clean white shirt. He ate breakfast, drank his coffee, then picked up his leather-bound ledger and his tin box and walked through the kitchen to a door that led to a section in the garage that served as his office. There men would come to elicit his help with their financial matters: taxes, budgets, and all manner of financial concerns.

My mother-in-law, Hattie Johnson, was just as meticulous and methodical in her routines as her husband, but she was far more personable and always had a warm and ready smile. Mother Johnson was a classic homemaker. She got up early every morning, made breakfast, and then spent her day cleaning, cooking, and baking bread. On laundry day, she washed her family's clothes in an old-style wringer washer and hung the sparkling clean laundry out to dry on a clothesline in the backyard. She treated her work lovingly, as though it were simply her daily work and not a chore.

Mother Johnson treated me like a daughter. She was kind to me. We talked about many things. She was a religious woman and was very concerned about the souls of her six children, and she cared about my religious health as well. One of her treasures was an old copy of *Ebony* magazine with a picture of a Black Jesus on the cover, which she kept on a bookcase in the living room. *Ebony* was a rather young publication at the time, its first issue published only six years before in 1945. We were all proud of this magazine whose purpose was to address African American issues, personalities, and interests in a positive and self-affirming manner. But Mother Johnson questioned the authenticity of Jesus as a Black man. Back then, there weren't many people who considered that Jesus could be anything but white. It was common knowledge that he was born and lived in the Middle East where people have dark skin, but the only pictures we saw of him depicted him as a white man. The reality that Jesus most likely had dark skin escaped us.

Chuck was not a regular churchgoer, and Mother Johnson wanted her son to be "saved" to ensure that there would be a place for him in Heaven when he passed away. I think she may have hoped that she could influence me to encourage him to attend church more regularly. She once said to me, "I would rather see him go even to the Catholic Church than not to be saved." I was taken aback for a moment and didn't know how to take her words. Having been born and raised Catholic, it had never occurred to me that some people viewed Catholicism as a substitute for what they considered to be "real" religion.

One evening when a visitor was leaving the Johnsons' home after an enjoyable evening, M.T. offered to drive him home. Mother Johnson climbed into the backseat so that M.T. and his friend could continue their conversation. For some reason, she stayed in the backseat after the friend got out of the car. While they were on their way home, a policeman stopped him. Then, as now, police randomly stopped Black men while they were driving—his appearance, character, or station in life did not matter. "Where you goin', boy?" the policeman demanded. He shined his flashlight through the car and stopped it briefly when it reached Mother Johnson's face. "Why is this white woman in your car?" he demanded. M.T. replied, "I was driving Miss Spears home." The policeman didn't need to know that the woman in the backseat, whose skin was so light that she was frequently mistaken for a white woman, was M.T.'s wife of many years. It was simply another example of how the police continually harassed us as well as an example of our creativity in avoiding conflict with them. From then on, the family jokingly called Mother Johnson "Miss Spears."

We left Texas in August 1951 and took a train to Boston. I remember that it took forever to get out of the state of Texas, but we seemed to travel through the other states rather quickly. We stopped in Washington, D.C., and spent a few days with Chuck's sister, Helen, and her husband, George Holland, whom I later learned was from St. Paul, Minnesota, and held a high level position in the federal government. This was two years before the Supreme Court's *District of Columbia v. John R. Thompson Co.* decision that would end segregation in Washington, D.C. restaurants, housing, businesses, and schools—a case that in many ways was a forerunner to *Brown v. Board of Education,* the landmark Supreme Court decision that ended segregation in public schools. Needless to say, things were already heating up there when we arrived.

We were very much aware that well-paying federal jobs had drawn a growing number of well-educated middle- and upper-income Black professionals and skilled workers to Washington, D.C. Chuck's brother-in-law worked in government finance and his sister was a teacher. We also knew that the city was deeply segregated and had some of the nation's worst living conditions, schools, and services in its African American neighborhoods.

In 1950, the year before our visit, Mary Church Terrell, an eighty-seven-year-old Black woman who chaired Washington's Coordinating Committee, had discovered along with attorneys in the Lawyers Guild that a number of laws from the Reconstruction Era that outlawed segregation had never been repealed. Mrs. Terrell led a small group into a restaurant called Thompson's Diner and requested a table. As expected, the manager promptly refused to serve them. The Coordinating Committee thrust the issue of segregated eating establishments onto the legal and social stage of the nation's capital. By the time Chuck and I arrived in D.C., the issue, while not resolved until two years later, in 1953, was already having positive effects; Blacks were getting far better services. I remember one day while I was waiting in line at a pharmacy the counter clerk, a Black woman, called me to the front of the line, deliberately ignoring the white customers who were ahead of me. While ringing up my order, she said, "Now I hope they understand what we have gone through all these years."

Helen and George were active in the changes that were happening in Washington, and they generously shared their knowledge with us, engaging us in constant conversations. Being with them reinforced what Chuck and I had learned while growing up and while we were students at Fisk. George was an older man and had been engaged in the struggle for a very long time. I remember him saying, "The thing that keeps me engaged is my clear understanding that every man puts his pants on the same way: one leg at a time." He believed that kind of realization kept him in the struggle and kept him believing that someday everyone would appreciate that fact. And it helped me continue to grow in my commitment to my people.

We stayed in Boston three years until Chuck was drafted into the U.S. Army. Our first year in Boston we stayed with a wonderful family from Arkansas, the Taylors, who welcomed us like we were members of their family. Their daughter, Alice Sanford, and I quickly became dear friends. We were in the same age group and were both college graduates. Alice went to Wellesley College, and we had many interesting conversations about our Southern backgrounds and family values. The differences in her Seven Sisters alma mater and my historically Black alma mater were the topic of many conversations.

Chuck and I had the misfortune of losing our first baby a couple of months after our arrival in Boston. My recovery from the miscarriage was slow, and I was in Massachusetts General Hospital for a long time. The Taylors were so kind to me during that difficult time. My mother was unable to travel because of her heart condition. Alice's husband was in the service by then so Alice was able to spend time with me. Mother was so grateful that I had found such a loving family to nurture her daughter in her absence.

Once I recovered, I found employment as a computer operator in Harvard University's aircraft experimental lab, reviewing recordings of flight maneuvers. I worked there for a year and then in a computer lab at MIT for another year, helping to introduce new users to computers. I also worked at Polaroid as an administrative assistant for a brief period. Looking back, I think now that I should have bought stock in Polaroid. Their cameras were innovative at the time and very popular.

In the years leading up to *Brown v. Board of Education,* there was turmoil regarding school desegregation in cities all across the nation. Boston was one of those cities. Its schools were deeply segregated, just like schools in the South. Black parents wanted to get their children into schools with the best resources for educational growth: smaller class sizes, up-to-date books, good school buildings, and quality teachers. Those schools were in white neighborhoods, particularly in South Boston, a neighborhood known to be deeply racist. In 1953, I was elected president of the Iota chapter, the graduate chapter of Delta Sigma Theta in Cambridge, and we were very active helping Black families with this new directive regarding school desegregation. We worked with parents to help them understand what a ruling would mean. We studied transportation and other issues of what quality education would look like for their children.

The Supreme Court ruled that school segregation was unconstitutional on May 17, 1954. Two weeks later, on June 2, Chuck and I were blessed with our firstborn daughter, Patrice Yvonne.

We left Massachusetts in July 1954, when Patrice was almost two months old. Chuck's graduate studies at MIT had led to a teaching fellowship at the University of Michigan. But just when we were about to move to Ann Arbor, he was drafted into the Army. Because of his expertise in engineering and mathematics, the Army stationed him at the Los Alamos National Atomic Laboratory in New Mexico. Los Alamos is best known as the site of the Manhattan Project, the research and development project that produced the first nuclear weapons during World War II.

The weather in Los Alamos was unusual to us. It was hot, dry, and windy in the daytime and very cold at night. I remember that laundry I hung out to dry was covered in sand when I brought it back inside. Chuck was very concerned about how the baby and I would fare in that climate, so we decided that it would be best for Patrice and me to stay in Houston with my parents. Los Alamos was close enough to Houston that he was able to visit frequently, for a few days every month or so. I decided that since I would be in Houston for the two years that Chuck was in the service, I would take some courses at Texas Southern University (TSU).

Texas Southern is an important institution both historically and for my family. My father and brother Judson Jr. both served on its Board of Trustees, and my other brother, Jim, earned his law degree there thirty years after my father had been denied his dream of studying law. Today, TSU is one of the largest and most comprehensive historically Black colleges in the nation and one of only four independent public universities in Texas. It has the distinction of being the only historically Black university in Texas, recognized by *Forbes* magazine as one of America's top colleges. It is the leading producer of college degrees among African Americans and Hispanics in Texas and ranks fourth in the United States in doctoral and professional degrees conferred to African Americans. But that was not always the case.

In 1927, the Houston school board established separate junior colleges because the state's public facilities were segregated. The board created two colleges, Houston Junior College and Houston Colored Junior College. The main provision of the authorization was that the colored college would need to meet all of its instructional expenses from tuition fees.

The first classes were held on summer evenings at Jack Yates High School, where my brothers would later go and graduate from. Enrollment that first summer was three hundred. The number dropped to eighty-eight students in the fall because many of the summer students were teachers who had to return to their jobs once the school year began. Nevertheless, the Houston Colored Junior College progressed fast, and by 1931, it was approved for accreditation by the Southern Association of Colleges and Schools.

Three years later, in the summer of 1934, the school board changed the junior college to a four-year college and changed its name to Houston College for Negroes. The first class of sixty-three students graduated in 1936. The college was able to add a graduate program in 1943. Two years later, the school district severed its relationship, and management of the college was vested in a newly developed Board of Regents. The college continued to operate at Yates High School, but by 1946 it had grown to an enrollment of approximately fourteen hundred students and needed room to grow. With the help of local philanthropist Hugh Roy

Cullen, the college obtained a fifty-three-acre piece of property in the Third Ward. Then, with the support of two sets of large donors, Mrs. T. M. Fairchild and Mr. and Mrs. C. A. Dupree, along with the African American community, the college raised enough money to construct the first building on its new campus. The college moved to its first building, the T. M. Fairchild Building, in 1946.

That same year, an African American mail carrier named Heman Marion Sweatt applied to enroll in the law school at the University of Texas. He was denied admission due to segregation and later, with the support of the NAACP, filed *Sweatt v. Painter*, a lawsuit against the University of Texas and the State of Texas. Believing the separate but equal doctrine would carry the day, the Texas Legislature passed Senate Bill 140 on March 3, 1947, providing for the establishment of a Negro law school in Houston and the creation of a university to surround it. This bill was complemented by House Bill 788, which approved $2 million to purchase a site near Houston to house this new college and support its operation.

Texas lawmakers initially considered Prairie View A&M College, the college my parents graduated from in the 1920s, as the location of the new law school. However, on June 14, 1947, two months before I left for Fisk University, the decision was made to use the site of Houston College for Negroes, with its new campus at the center of a large and fast-growing black population. Thus the Texas State University for Negroes was born. The new university was charged with teaching "pharmacy, dentistry, arts and sciences, journalism, education, literature, law, medicine, and other professional courses." The legislature stipulated that "these courses shall be equivalent to those offered at other institutions of this type supported by the State of Texas." In 1951, the name was permanently changed to Texas Southern University.

• • •

Initially, my plan was to go to the School of Social Work at TSU. But somewhere along the line, I decided instead to take courses in the department of education where I was able to focus on the educational needs of Black children and theories ascribed to learning. I became deeply interested in education and decided to get a teaching certificate. I'm not sure what influenced that decision. Being married with a small child may have played into it, because I would be able to complete a program within the two-year time frame that Chuck would be in the service. My mother's passion for educating our children was certainly also an influence. The nursery school she opened when I graduated from high school had been identified as a model for nursery school teachers, and as it turned out TSU students who were studying early childhood education did their practice teaching there.

By the time I returned to Houston with Patrice, my parents were well established in Pleasantville. Mother continued to work daily, managing the project, in spite of her heart condition. She was fortunate to have hired Marie Taulton, a woman who in spirit, love, and support became like family. Marie took care of Mother and her home. When I moved in with my parents, she also helped with Patrice. By the time Mother and I felt that Patrice and I were settled enough, Patrice knew Marie well and loved her. I felt so blessed. She was the sweetest person and a wonderful babysitter. She made it possible for me to go to school. I could leave home after nursing the baby and I knew Marie would take care of Patrice and my parents' house. I was able to complete my courses and my practice teaching without worry.

After Chuck was discharged from the Army and we left Houston, I always made sure to look in on Marie and her sisters whenever we went home to visit. I remember how devastated I was when her sisters told me one visit that Marie had died tragically. She had gotten obese as she grew older and had died in a fire in her home, in part because she was unable to escape the house to safety. The tragic death of the woman who had been so kind and loving to my mother and Patrice was beyond belief.

The environment of activism at Texas Southern and in Houston culture in general was strong, and being steeped in that culture in that particular moment in history was very meaningful to me. I spent a lot of time with fellow graduate students and Houston friends discussing current events, hearing Thurgood Marshall's lectures again, and discussing the Supreme Court school desegregation decision. The courage of Rosa Parks and the determination of the people who participated in the Montgomery bus boycott reinforced the sense of possibility that my parents had instilled in me as a child, which was solidified at Fisk—the hope that we as a people would someday achieve freedom and equality.

I completed my teaching certificate in June 1956 and our second daughter, Norrene Elaine, was born on October 8. This was shortly before Chuck was discharged from the Army, and I laugh when I remember the day my brother said to him, "You're almost out of the Army and you have a family. You're going to have a find a job, man." It wasn't long after that Chuck applied to Honeywell in Minnesota and was hired as a research engineer/mathematician. And so when Patrice was two years old and Norrene was just six weeks, we packed up and moved to Minneapolis.

4

MINNEAPOLIS

CHUCK WAS THE THIRD BLACK PROFESSIONAL ever hired at Honeywell. The first was nuclear physicist Woodfin Lewis and the second was Luther Prince, an electrical engineer. Chuck had met Luther when they were graduate students at MIT. Woody Lewis and his wife, Virginia, we knew, were Fisk alumni.

When Chuck came to Minneapolis for his interview with Honeywell, he also met Oscar and Ora Newman—Ora worked at Honeywell and Oscar worked at the nuclear plant in Anoka. Oscar's father was Cecil E. Newman, the founder and publisher of the *Minneapolis Spokesman* and the *St. Paul Recorder,* the first Black newspapers in Minnesota, and he was the first president of the Minneapolis Urban League. Cecil was a prominent leader among Black Minnesotans. He was active on corporate boards and in political circles and was close friends with Hubert H. Humphrey. We were also very close with two other prominent journalists, Carl T. Rowan and his wife, Vivien. At the time, Carl was a columnist for the *Minneapolis Star Tribune,* one of a very few Black journalists to hold such a position for a major newspaper. Another friend was Mary Kyle, founder and publisher of the *St. Paul Courier.* She later became publisher of the *St. Paul Recorder* and would later travel with me to Jackson, Mississippi, during the Wednesdays in Mississippi movement in Freedom Summer in 1964.

The Newmans became our Minneapolis family. They helped us get settled and oriented to our new home. They were well connected in the Twin Cities community, including its politics and social life, and introduced us to a large group of Black professionals. And when our youngest daughter, Josie Irene, was born two years after we moved to Minneapolis, the Newmans and Katie McWatt became her godparents.

It was exciting, as we settled into our new community, to meet so many young, professionally trained, and interesting Black families: doctors who practiced at the University of Minnesota Hospital and taught at the University Medical School; teachers and social workers who introduced creative strategies for developing a curriculum and effective methods for teaching Black children their history in the Minneapolis Public Schools; and individuals who would make significant political and social contributions to the community. One of the doctors we became friends with was Cassius Ellis and his wife, Phyllis. Cassius delivered Josie. What a day that was. Chuck was in Wilmington, Delaware, for Honeywell when I went into labor. I called Dr. Ellis and then the Newmans. Oscar came right away and took Patrice and Norrene to stay with him and Ora, and Cassius took me to the University of Minnesota Hospital. He must have called Honeywell and left a message for Chuck to catch the next plane home. The plane didn't arrive until after Josie was born, so when Oscar met Chuck at the airport, he said, "You have a beautiful, healthy baby girl."

Some of our other new friends were Archie Givens Sr., the first Black millionaire in Minnesota, and his wife, Phebe; and architect Lorenzo "Pete" Williams and his wife, Lillian, who would later become the founding director of the University of Minnesota's Office of Equal Opportunity and Affirmative Action. Richard and Jean Fox and their daughters also became like family to us. When we met them, Richard was working for the Minnesota State Commission against Discrimination. He later became U.S. Ambassador to Trinidad and Tobago under the Carter Administration.

We also became great friends with St. Paul activists Katie McWatt, her husband, Arthur, known as Chan, and their children. Chan was an author and a history teacher in the St. Paul Public Schools and Katie became like a sister to me. Our community interests merged in many ways. We frequently saw parallels in our strategies in our community efforts and often collaborated together to address them. We became known as counterparts—she was often called "St. Paul's Josie Johnson" whereas I was "Minneapolis's Katie McWatt."

Katie became director of the St. Paul Urban League and was the first Black candidate to run for St. Paul City Council. After retiring from the Urban League, she became adviser to African American students at St. Paul Central High. She exposed the students to African American history and escorted them on trips to historic Black colleges when they were deciding where to apply upon graduation.

Many of the women in our group of friends met monthly to play bridge. I very much enjoyed their company even though I didn't think I was smart enough to learn to play bridge. We talked about many things as they too were aware of issues that needed to be addressed in our communities, both in Minnesota and nationwide. For instance, when Chuck and I moved to Minneapolis, Black people were less than 3 percent of the population and lived in limited sections on the North and South Sides and in St. Paul. The women helped me become grounded in the observations I was making about housing and other issues that affected us. For instance, Black Minneapolitans were deeply aware that we would be in danger if we dared to go to Northeast Minneapolis.

In turn, I shared with them the results of the *Brown v. Board of Education* decision that I witnessed while living with my family in Houston when Chuck was in the Army. Before *Brown v. Board of Education,* schools in Houston were named after Black historical figures such as Booker T. Washington and Houston educator Ernest Ollington Smith, and skilled Black teachers taught our children in those schools. But after the decision, many of our schools were renamed and those great teachers were moved to white schools or demoted to administrative positions. They were replaced by young, white, newly graduated teachers who were assigned to Black schools. The white female teachers were intimidated by Black male high school students; having no understanding of the young men's ways of being, they allowed them to behave in ways that the Black teachers would never have allowed. They didn't encourage the boys to listen to their instruction but instead allowed them to get up from their seats and move around the classroom and sometimes accused the boys of flirting with them. That was the beginning of a terrible decline in the education of our children that exists to this day. On a more positive note, my new friends and I shared the pride we felt about the Montgomery bus boycott that had ended shortly before Chuck and I moved to Minneapolis.

Not long before we moved to Minneapolis, a group of nineteen Southern Senators and seventy-seven members of the House of Representatives signed what they called the Southern Manifesto, a resolution condemning *Brown v. Board of Education.* The resolution called the decision "a clear abuse of judicial power" and encouraged states to resist implementing its mandates. Over the following year, I had many conversations with family and friends, including the women in the bridge group, about the Supreme Court's decision as well as the negative reactions to it. The day when the students whom history would dub the Little Rock Nine were scheduled to integrate Central High School in Little Rock, Arkansas, is still as fresh in my mind as the day it happened. It was September 4, 1957, and I was at home with Norrene, who was almost a year old. I sat in front of the television holding little Norrene on my lap and watched in astonishment as a white mob gathered in front of the school and Governor Orval Faubus stood at the front door to block the way so those young people couldn't enter. Women spat on the teens and threatened them. How, I wondered, could those women, many of whom were mothers, treat those children that way?

Through our many new connections, we learned that Minnesota had quite an interesting political history regarding African Americans. As I became more knowledgeable about Minnesota's history of denying Blacks the right to vote, hold political office, and serve on juries, it became increasingly clear that we had a lot of work ahead of us. Discrimination was not limited to the Southern states. I learned about the Minnesota legend, scholar, lawyer, and legislator J. Francis Wheaton. During his one term in office, Representative Wheaton introduced fifteen bills. Chief among them was an amendment to an 1885 civil rights bill that prevented businesses from refusing service to anyone on the basis of race or color. Wheaton proposed an addition that made the list of pertinent businesses exhaustive. The bill passed both the House and Senate and was signed into law by Governor John Lind on March 6, 1899.

Nearly eighty more years passed before another Black would be elected to a Minnesota state office. That man was our veterinarian and dear friend Dr. B. Robert Lewis, the first Black man to be elected to the Minnesota State Senate. Bob was elected in 1972 but unfortunately passed away in 1979 during his second term in office. In 1983, the University of Minnesota School of Veterinary Medicine named its hospital for companion animals in his name. It was the first time the university had named a facility after a Black person. Also, because of legislation he authored to aid women in

abusive relationships and stem domestic violence, two battered women's shelters in Minnesota (in Eagan and Hastings)
bear his name. In 1973, Ray Pleasant was the second Black
person elected to the State Legislature. In 2001, Neva Walker
became the first Black woman and Muslim to be elected to
the Minnesota House of Representatives.

In our early days in Minnesota, we also learned that as
mayor of Minneapolis from 1945–48, Hubert H. Humphrey
had worked hard to eliminate discrimination and bigotry in
all of its forms. Chuck and I were quite shocked to learn that
in addition to deep-seated racism Minneapolis was widely
known as the anti-Semitic capital of America. Before coming
here, we had no idea that there was such bigotry in Minnesota:
its reputation was that it was a friendly, liberal environment.

Humphrey was well known for his public speaking style
and his liberal philosophy. In 1948, he attracted national attention with an impassioned speech at the Democratic National
Convention, in which he argued that the party's presidential
platform should include a civil rights plank. In the race for
a U.S. Senate seat that fall, Humphrey's populist-style coalition of Democrats, farmers, and labor unions propelled him
to victory in Minnesota, a state that had not elected a Democratic senator since 1901. He continued his battle throughout
his long career, establishing Human Rights Commissions and
encouraging participation to eliminate discrimination in the
city of Minneapolis.

Among the many people who became our close friends
shortly after our arrival to Minneapolis was William Matthew Little. Matthew grew up in Washington, D.C., and following military service in World War II he earned a degree
in biological science from North Carolina A&T, a historic
Black university located in Greensboro. But he learned the
limitations of fairness and justice in Minneapolis soon after he
came here on a fluke in 1948. After graduating from college,
he had moved to Milwaukee to work in an auto body plant.

But he didn't like Milwaukee, so one day he packed his bags and went to the railroad station. He wasn't sure where he would end up; when the clerk asked where he wanted to go, two places came to mind. He flipped a coin—heads for Minneapolis, tails for Denver. The coin came up heads and he boarded the next train headed for Minneapolis.

Apparently, the bills that J. Frank Wheaton introduced back in 1899 hadn't lasted, because when Matt Little arrived in Minneapolis, he was surprised to find that, much like the Jim Crow South, Blacks were not allowed to stay in major hotels and unwritten rules among employers kept them from many jobs. He had long desired to be a fire fighter, but his application to the all-white Minneapolis Fire Department fell flat even though he scored top grades on the exams. When he asked why he wasn't hired, he was told that firefighters live in close quarters. "I don't think that's going to work," said one of the men who interviewed him. He became disillusioned and very angry because he thought Minnesota would be a place where this kind of discrimination did not exist.

The fiasco with the Minneapolis Fire Department was the final straw in a series of events that spurred what would become Matthew's lifelong commitment to civil rights. He created a successful lawn care service to earn a living for himself and his family and devoted his life to civil rights issues. He was president of the Minneapolis NAACP when we moved to Minneapolis. He invited me to join the board and accept the role of treasurer. He also gave me the history of his efforts in the fight against housing and other inequities practiced in the Twin Cities. Deep patterns of injustice were well established by the time we arrived. Being deeply involved in the struggles of our people, I always found myself drawn in the direction of service to my community, no matter where I lived. I gladly accepted Matt's invitation to join the board of the Minneapolis NAACP. I was eager to begin serving the Twin Cities community.

• • •

When I became active in Minneapolis, I learned so much about the work that had been accomplished for civil rights long before our arrival. For instance, the work that Hubert H. Humphrey had done as mayor, followed by his successor, Orville Freeman, to create a local fair employment practices ordinance that paved the way for the law that was later adopted nationally. I felt incredibly blessed to find that the Twin Cities was a community where things could be done. I also joined the Urban League. Chuck joined as well and later became a member of its board of directors. Along with several other men among our group of friends, he and Pete Williams helped form the Monitors, a club whose purpose was to provide African American men with financial investment skills and civic opportunities.

At the same time we became very good friends with Celia Logan, a white woman who was one of Chuck's colleagues at Honeywell. Celia loved nature and viewed it as part of her spiritual life. We spent much time with her learning about birds, flowers, rocks, and trees. After living in South Minneapolis for seven years, Chuck and I purchased a home in Bloomington in 1962. Our new home was near a pond with a stream that ran at the end of our property. I looked out my window one day and saw a strange and beautiful bird, the likes of which I had never seen before. It was large and graceful and was perched on a rock. I called Celia and described it to her. She wasn't busy so she drove to our home to see if she could identify it for me. I was afraid it would leave before she arrived, but it was still there, sitting very still on the same rock. "It's a great blue heron," she said and proceeded to tell me everything she knew about the majestic bird.

Celia also introduced me to the League of Women Voters and to Alpha Smaby, who was a very strong political personality at the time. Alpha was a farsighted woman and a strong outspoken person for women's rights and social justice. Later, she would serve two terms in the Minnesota House of Representatives. Florence Gray was president of the Minneapolis League at the time, and she immediately engaged me. I was soon appointed to the Minneapolis board; Florence and I developed a very close friendship. We traveled together and shared much about our African American and Jewish cultural histories. One trip I remember well was to the offices of *Ebony* magazine in Chicago where we had a wonderfully engaging meeting with John H. Johnson, its founder and publisher. I also became close friends with Barbara Stuhler, an author, historian, civic leader, and professor at the University of Minnesota who also served on the National Board of the League of Women Voters. Several years after I joined the Minneapolis League, Barbara nominated me for a position on the national board. I was the first Black woman to hold an office on the Minneapolis board of the League of Women Voters and the first to serve on its national board.

The League of Women Voters was my source for nonpartisan and scholarly studies of government. I learned the structure and processes of city, state, and federal government and Minnesota politics. Their research, reporting, and balanced approach to issues provided me with the basis for understanding the process I needed when I became a lobbyist for the issues I would work on later in the 1960s.

My three daughters were very young when I began volunteering for the NAACP and the League of Women Voters. In order to be effective with my family and my community, I planned meals carefully and only shopped twice a month. And I took my children to meetings with me, where they sat under tables and read books or played with their toys while I engaged in important discussions and planning. I still smile when I think of little Norrene asking for "juice without fishes," which is what she called orange juice without pulp. Chuck was very supportive of my volunteer activities and, like my own father, he gave our children his full attention, helping with their homework and engaging them in conversation. We didn't go on many vacations. The only one I recall was when we took a road trip to Texas and Massachusetts to show our girls where we came from and what our lives were like before they were born. We did however go on day trips to nearby places such as the Wisconsin Dells, and we always went to the State Fair.

It could be said that my relationship with the University of Minnesota began at this same time because Chuck and I enrolled Patrice and Norrene in the University of Minnesota preschool. There, our circle of friends expanded and I met my dear friend Sarah Roberson. Sarah and I carpooled to the nursery school, and my daughters became friends with her daughter and son. My girls made many other friends there as well. Little did I know at the time that the university would become the center of my social, academic, and professional life many years later.

Shortly after I became involved with the Minneapolis NAACP and the League of Women Voters, Robert Williams, then executive director of the Urban League, invited me to accept the position of community organizer for the League. Things were pretty formal in the 1950s and 1960s, and married women still used their husbands' names. In fact, the *Minneapolis Star Tribune* referred to me as Mrs. Charles Johnson in an article they published about my community activities and family life. The formality of those times caused Williams to suggest having a formal meeting with my husband to discuss the possibility of hiring me. The meeting was quite positive, but Chuck made it very clear to Mr. Williams that he could afford to support his family and I didn't need that job. His mother didn't work and he wanted to be sure that it was known that if his wife worked, it wasn't because her income was needed. And I accepted the position.

5

THE URBAN LEAGUE
AND FIGHTING FOR
FAIR HOUSING

A LOT WAS HAPPENING in the late 1950s that suggested change was on its way. But as the years went on, it became clear that the changes we hoped for would be hard won. The landmark *Brown v. Board of Education* in 1954 was an effort to settle the question of whether or not Blacks and whites could receive an equal education, either integrated with or separate from each other, by overturning the U.S. Supreme Court *Plessy v. Ferguson* case of 1896, which had established the separate-but-equal doctrine. The *Plessy v. Ferguson* case stemmed from an incident in 1892: an African American train passenger named Homer Plessy refused to sit in a Jim Crow car, breaking a Louisiana law, and was brought before Judge John H. Ferguson of the Criminal Court for New Orleans. Judge Ferguson rejected Plessy's argument that his constitutional rights were violated and ruled that a state law that "implies merely a legal distinction between whites and Blacks did not conflict with the 13th and 14th Amendments." Restrictive legislation based on race continued until the *Brown v. Board of Education* case.

For me, acceptance of the community organizer position at the Minneapolis Urban League was a way to contribute to the change we hoped for. I have great respect for this organization since my father was a founding member of the

Houston Area Urban League. The National Urban League was formed in 1910 to help Black people who were moving from the South to the North to get the services they needed in their new communities—such as employment, housing, health care, and education. The Minneapolis affiliate saw its role as continuing to honor that mission for individuals and families who were moving to Minneapolis, and the community organizer's responsibility was to help find viable solutions to these problems. There was a pattern of neighborhood segregation in Minneapolis, and schools reflected this pattern. *Brown v. Board of Education* added a degree of focus to the agency's work in desegregating Minneapolis schools.

Much of my focus as community organizer would be on the agency's education mission. In the early 1960s before I was hired, one of my major volunteer missions was education. I volunteered in K–8 schools helping to organize parent advocate programs. I met with teachers and parents to teach them Black history and to help parents become better advocates for their children. We experimented with a variety of strategies to get parents involved; we held the meetings in the evenings and arranged taxi service and offered stipends. Something I learned during that experience was that a lot of the parents had negative experiences in school that deeply contributed to how they viewed teachers and their own children's educational possibilities. For this and perhaps other reasons, the program was effective and gave participating parents a more positive view of how they could help their children obtain the best possible education in Minneapolis public schools. I believe the concept of parent advocacy still exists in some form.

Once I began my position, one of the first things I learned was that our community had many issues for which help was needed after the office closed. Often, just as I was about to leave for the day, several people would come in seeking help with finding food or shelter for the night, or asking where they could go to get help with a health-related problem. I was very concerned. There had to be a way to respond. I investigated resources that were available in our community for those after-hours emergencies. One method I employed was to keep the office open after our regular hours so that I could receive and welcome people who were in need, tell them where the resources were, and to take them there, if necessary. Chuck was very helpful and understanding, and our children accepted that our dinnertime was 8 p.m.

The people who needed after-hours services represented the population the Urban League was organized to help: African Americans who had been living in this community for a long time as well as those who were moving here from other places, both urban and rural, but all of whom were seeking needed assistance to adjust to their new community. New residents came from Los Angeles, Chicago, Detroit, and cities in Mississippi, Louisiana, as well as other locations. Over time, it was revealed that social workers in cities across the country had learned that Minnesota welcomed newcomers and treated them more humanely than they were treated in other states and were encouraging clients to come here.

I felt it was important to know which places could help with each particular service and to build relationships with directors of those services so we could get the help our clients needed. I spent much time developing relationships with directors of shelters, food shelves, and churches. And because of the needs our people were experiencing and the Urban League's limited resources, I encouraged Robert to campaign to have us included among the agencies to receive contributions from the United Way. He did apply and we were soon placed on the United Way's Community Fund, which allowed us to provide more services.

• • •

Shortly after my transition to becoming a full-time Urban League employee, I lost my beloved mother. This was the most significant and painful experience in my life up to that point. It was Saturday, May 21, 1960. I was twenty-nine. We were all at home when the call came. I don't remember if it was my father or one of my brothers who called, but he said Mother had died. Mother had been helping a friend prepare a wedding shower for her daughter when she had a heart attack. Her heart was damaged from her childhood rheumatic fever, but that had never stopped her from being of service to others. She was taken home and died shortly after. I was devastated. I nearly fell apart from the shock and disbelief. I still feel her loss as freshly as I did the day she died.

She was only fifty-three years old, and we were very close. Mother was my very best friend: our spirits were so in tune that I usually knew when she was not feeling well. How could she be gone? And my poor father—he too was in disbelief and seemed so helpless. I remember Chuck saying to the girls, "Let's let Mother have time to herself," taking them into another room, which allowed me to grieve for as long as I needed to. Then he made preparations for the girls and me to take a train to Houston for Mother's arrangements and her funeral.

My daughters would never get to know their grand-mother, as her poor health limited her from traveling very far from Houston, San Antonio, or Crockett, Texas, where she could visit my grandmother and other family members. The girls' only memory of her is the one time my parents came to visit us in Minnesota. They traveled by train because Mother was unable to fly. The trip was exhausting for her. The restrictions she had to live with caused her much sad-ness. While they were here, I took her to the University of Minnesota Heart Hospital to find out if they could repair the hole in her heart. Unfortunately, they were not able to.

Baby Josie Irene was only a few months old when my

parents visited. I remember that we drove up to Duluth and took them to a park. Mother and Dad were impressed by the beauty in Minnesota but were surprised that it was so cold in the month of August. Dad was also surprised that there were so few Black people in our South Minneapolis neighbor-hood. Coming from Houston, Dad was used to seeing Blacks everywhere. One day he went for a walk. He was gone so long that we began to worry. When he returned he said, "I found them." He was delighted to have seen more Black people. We got a big charge out of his expression.

I missed my mother's daily calls—our conversations had helped ground me in my work. I was glad to get back to my community work with the Urban League after we returned from her funeral. In some small ways, being able to resume my focus on community organizing was helpful because I was continuing her legacy of working with our community. I had also become deeply involved with the Democratic–Farmer–Labor (DFL) Party by then. I was elected precinct chair and was busy attending the State Central Committee meetings as well as League of Women Voters' meetings. I remember sit-ting with Walter "Fritz" Mondale one day in 1960 when he was called to Governor Orville Freeman's office. Miles Lord had resigned his position of Attorney General in order to accept an appointment as the U.S. Attorney for the District of Minnesota. Governor Freeman called Fritz to his office to offer him the position of Attorney General. Those politi-cal activities helped soften the blow of not being able to talk with Mother every day as we had done since I left home for college thirteen years before.

As we entered the 1960s, issues of equality for Black people in Minnesota became more and more apparent and began to take on a stronger sense of urgency. We began drawing parallels between the issues facing our people in the South and in Minnesota—in terms of employment, education, and housing. Hubert H. Humphrey and Orville Freeman, his successor, had made progress in their efforts toward fair employment but fair housing proved to be a more difficult and personal issue.

I became involved in the efforts to pass a Fair Housing Bill in Minnesota in 1959. I had had an opportunity to be engaged with various groups working to gather evidence of discrimination in the showing and selling of properties; in the practice of redlining by lending institutions; and in false claims regarding a fair housing law in Minnesota. I had been an active member of groups that had been testing patterns of housing discrimination by sending Blacks and whites to lending institutions and rental agencies to see who would be accepted and rejected for housing loans and rental units. Time and time again, Black families were either rejected for rental units and loans or offered inflated loans higher than those offered to whites.

During the 1961 legislative session, once again the history of efforts by politicians, religious and spiritual organizations, and social and community groups was reviewed and groups reassembled to get a Fair Housing Bill passed in the Minnesota State Legislature. The history of the effort was reported and supported by the press—every angle, including correcting misinformation, was publically reported. The Minneapolis and St. Paul Urban League directors, Robert Williams and Ernest Cooper, testified in a joint statement before the House Committee regarding the status of housing opportunities for Black citizens in the Twin Cities. They presented statistics on where Black citizens lived in the two cities and identified the effect of the construction of I-94 and the need to relocate the Black Rondo community. They reported the fact that Minneapolis had two Black residential communities, one each on the south and north sides of the city, and that adequate rental housing was "almost nonexistent." Their report added urgency to the need for fairness in housing opportunities for Blacks in Minnesota.

Something else we learned was that in Minneapolis and St. Paul, as in much of the rest of the country, Blacks were contending with the vestiges of the racial covenants written into the deeds for many residential properties, which often stated that the property could not be rented or sold to any member of the "Negro race." While the Supreme Court had declared in the 1948 case *Shelley v. Kraemer* that the covenants were no longer enforceable, they had created informal patterns of discrimination in the Twin Cities that continued well into the 1960s.

Williams and my dear friend Richard "Dick" Fox encouraged me to lobby for passage of the Fair Housing Bill. Somehow Dick was always able to find space for me to work in his office at the MN Fair Employment Practices Commission. I remember joking that he pulled a desk and chair from the ceiling whenever I came to work. I accepted the role of chief lobbyist for this effort and was able to convince my friends Katie McWatt, Matt Little, and Zetta Feder to join me. We became full-time, unpaid lobbyists during the 1961 legislative session. We spent long hours at the State Capitol meeting with legislators, answering their questions, and lobbying on behalf of the bill. Our interactions with them made it clear to us that many legislators had very limited exposure to Black or Jewish people. The legislators soon learned that we knew the details of the housing bill before they did and that we knew, from personal experience, the issues at the heart of the legislation.

Many years later, in conversation with my friend and colleague Geri Joseph, I was reminded that in the early days of the 1960s, the DFL—in its conscious awareness and its efforts to address diversity and justice issues—was open to newcomers. I myself was a newcomer then, and it was observed that I appeared to be friendly yet straightforward, committed, and unafraid to suggest strategies and ideas without being hostile or overly demanding. Perhaps those attributes were what made the legislators listen to me, even if they disagreed with fair housing.

In the spring of 1961, as this legislative battle was reaching a climax, the bill was held up in the Senate Judiciary Committee. Senator Donald Fraser, who would later serve two terms as mayor of Minneapolis, was convinced that the bill would die there. However, I thought that Governor Elmer Andersen might be able to help. I had met him and knew his attitude about justice and fairness. He was a Republican and was newly elected and had already offered clear support for fair housing. I knew that he was not a newcomer to civil rights issues: when he had been a senator representing a St. Paul district, he had been a staunch advocate for the state law banning job discrimination, enacted in 1955.

I went to Governor Andersen and told him that the bill was in danger. As I expected, he was indeed concerned. He offered me a seat in his office and wrote this note to the Judiciary Committee:

To: Members of the Senate Judiciary Committee

Dear Senator:

May I respectfully request your favorable consideration of S.F. 750, the Fair Housing bill. I write so you will be informed of my unqualified support of this legislation if that should be a factor in your final decision.

The opposition involves the same arguments as were used against FEPC [Fair Employment Practice Committee], none of which materialized.

The great plus in supporting legislation to eliminate discrimination is that it shows our willingness to implement with legislation our belief in equality. I know we cannot legislate attitudes into people's minds, but we can legislate

against injustice. I am not sure we always realize the sig-
nificance to all the world of our actions as individuals and
state legislatures in matters of this kind.
     I hope you will vote for the bill.

     Sincerely yours,

     Elmer L. Andersen
     GOVERNOR

I took the note to Senator Fraser and, with the help and direct engagement of Governor Andersen, got the bill out of the Senate Judiciary Committee. It passed by one vote and then went to the full Senate. Senator Fraser and Representative Robert Latz were convinced that without the help of the governor it would not have passed. Minnesota was the first state in the nation to pass a fair housing bill. President Lyndon B. Johnson signed the Civil Rights Act in 1964 and, four years later, in 1968, the Fair Housing Act.

The year after the Civil Rights Act was passed, author Sam Greenlee released a novel, *The Spook Who Sat by the Door,* about the first Black CIA agent whose role was to sit quietly in full view of anyone who passed by the office. Although the book is highly charged because of its premise of Black people taking matters into their own hands following the assassinations of Dr. Martin Luther King Jr., Malcolm X, President John F. Kennedy, and Robert Kennedy, I couldn't help remembering with amusement the day I sat in Governor Andersen's office while he composed that amazingly effective note that caused the Fair Housing Bill to be passed.

6

THE MARCH
ON WASHINGTON

IN THE EARLY 1960S, civil rights activists like A. Philip Randolph began to evaluate early efforts to improve the rights and quality of life for Black Americans in education, employment, and justice. Randolph and a group of colleagues recorded the struggle of the labor union movement to advance economic justice and collected data regarding job discrimination. Key questions they asked: Had *Brown v. Board of Education* really made a difference in the education of African American children? Did the FEPC protect Black Defense Department employees during the World War II? In 1941, Randolph and Bayard Rustin organized and planned a march on Washington as the next protest strategy, but Randolph had made agreements with President Roosevelt in the late 1930s and early '40s that resulted in canceling that civil rights march. It was not until 1963 and with much persistence from the leadership in the Black community that President Kennedy lent support to a civil rights march. Along with people all across the nation, we in Minnesota began making plans in the spring of 1963 to participate in the historic march on Washington. The national organizing committee was very much aware of Hubert H. Humphrey's powerful speech in 1948, which had established Minnesota as a state where civil rights were taken seriously. As president of the Minneapolis branch of the NAACP, Matthew Little was asked to coordinate the Minnesota delegation. Matt did not expect to be honored with such a daunting task and his initial thought was to say no. There were a lot of violent, horrible things happening to civil rights workers in the South, and he was worried about that happening in Washington. But his desire to serve our people won out. He asked me to assist him and Marjorie Wynn, who had called the first Minnesota group together to discuss the march, and we began making our plans. We consulted with local civil rights and religious groups to determine who should go and raised the $5,000 we would need to charter a plane for our delegation. Thankfully, the religious community generously helped us with that effort, as did many individuals—some of whom attended the march while others could not.

The national committee gave us strict instructions on how to handle ourselves. Everyone who attended had to sign a contract stating that they would remain nonviolent: we could not retaliate if we were attacked. I worried about the warnings that we were receiving, but it did not dissuade me from going. I wanted to be engaged in the mission of the march. Some people who had planned to join us declined to sign the contract, stating that they weren't sure they could be nonviolent if attacked. Nevertheless, they were willing to help us raise the funds to go. In addition, because the theme of the march centered on jobs and freedom, the national NAACP had other requirements as well. Each delegation had to include so many women, so many unemployed—individuals who were part of the groups that represented the issues we were fighting for. Thomas Johnson, a well-known medical doctor in our community, was one of the people who couldn't sign the pledge for fear that he wouldn't respond nonviolently if attacked. He donated his plane fare so that someone without means could join us.

We ended up with fifty-eight people in the Minnesota

delegation: Black people and white people, Christians and Jews, young people and older people, all of us making up a group that consisted of individuals who represented the issues behind the march. There were others who traveled separately by car, bus, train, or air and were not identified as part of the official Minnesota delegation. Our departure was scheduled for 3 a.m. on the morning of the march. I was late getting to the airport due to some last-minute family things but thankfully arrived just in time. I think I would have died if I had missed that trip. When I arrived at the airport, I saw Barbara Cyrus, one of our outstanding supporters and a writer for the *Minneapolis Spokesman,* who was there to wish us "God's safety and good luck." She wasn't able to go to D.C., but we all knew her heart was with us.

On the plane we sang freedom songs and discussed our excitement for the march as well as the frightening things that had occurred in the weeks leading up to the march: Alabama Governor George Wallace's vow to defend segregation forever; Dr. Martin Luther King's arrest; the dogs and hoses that were turned on civil rights workers; the assassination of activist Medgar Evers, who had been gunned down in his driveway; and the threats and attacks by neo-Nazi skinheads, which seemed to be going on everywhere. All of this added to our anxiety. We were nervous but more determined than ever.

When we arrived in Washington, D.C., we were escorted to waiting cars that drove us to First Congregational Church where we would be able to rest and eat breakfast before the march began. We were surprised to see that the streets were empty and silent. It was so quiet that we began to fear that the march was going to fail. At the church we were ushered into the basement. We freshened up and were soon joined by Minnesota dignitaries Hubert H. Humphrey, Don Fraser, and Eugene McCarthy, all who came to greet us and give us encouragement before the march began. Minneapolis mayor

Art Naftalin flew in with us and joined the group of welcoming Minnesota politicians when we arrived.

When we left the church and began walking toward the Lincoln Memorial reflecting pool, we were happily surprised to see that crowds of people were already there. It is well known that more than 250,000 people attended the march, making it the largest demonstration ever seen up to that time in the nation's capital, and one of the first to have extensive television coverage. We stepped in behind the large, boisterous New York delegation. We were blessed to have a bright sunny day, but it was so hot and humid that even in our excitement we couldn't help trying to find a shady spot once we made it to Lincoln Memorial.

Soon after we arrived, Marian Anderson began singing the national anthem, and the crowd joined in. We placed our right hands over our hearts and sang along, forgetting about looking for a shady spot. The program continued with a lovely invocation by the Very Reverend Patrick O'Boyle, Archbishop of Washington. A. Philip Randolph followed, reiterating why we were there—to stop discrimination and demand jobs and freedom for all. I couldn't help crying when Medgar Evers's widow, Myrlie, stepped up to the podium and gave a tribute to the women freedom fighters. She named Daisy Bates, Diane Nash-Bevel, Mrs. Herbert Lee, Rosa Parks, and Gloria Richardson, and as she spoke the women in the crowd gave a nod to the women who fought for freedom in our own communities. There were many other speakers—John Lewis, Walter Reuther, James Farmer, Rabbi Uri Miller, Whitney Young, Matthew Ahman, Roy Wilkins, Rabbi Joachim Prinz—interspersed with musical selections by the Eva Jessie choir. And then the program took an unexpected turn that would forever change the history of the march.

It is well documented that Dr. Martin Luther King Jr. and Mahalia Jackson, the Queen of Gospel, were friends, a friendship that began when Miss Jackson appeared in Montgomery, Alabama, at the request of Reverend Ralph Abernathy to support the bus boycott, the event that launched the civil rights movement. She had sung by Reverend King's side many times since that day, and by the time of the March on Washington, he had become quite comfortable telling her what to sing and she was just as comfortable suggesting directions that he should take in his speeches. So it was no surprise to anyone who knew them that he asked her to sing "I've Been 'Buked, and I've Been Scorned" to lead into his speech at the march.

When she finished the song, Miss Jackson took her seat directly behind Dr. King and listened while he spoke. At a critical point during his speech, she decided to intervene. Recalling a theme she had heard him use in his earlier speeches, Miss Jackson said out loud, "Tell them about your dream, Martin." Films of this speech show that at that moment Dr. King left his notes behind and improvised the next part of his speech—the historic section that is still lauded today.

I don't think anyone expected the type of speech Dr. King delivered that day, or the lasting impact it would have across the nation and the world. I began to cry, and when I looked around I saw tears flowing from many eyes as far as I could see as the crowd felt the impact of his words. Soon after the march, President Kennedy called segregation immoral and began paving the way for a comprehensive civil rights bill, which would clear several hurdles in Congress and go on to win the endorsement of House and Senate Republican leaders that fall.

Another of the national committee's instructions was that marchers were to leave Washington before sundown, for our safety. But the feelings of joy and hope stayed with us. We felt that we really could change the laws and make a difference for our people. Upon our return to Minnesota, our delegation organized a local March on Washington committee. The intent of the committee was to follow up on the placards carried during the march—jobs, housing, education, and so on—and to be cognizant of efforts in our state honoring the promise of the march.

One Friday in November 1963, the week before Thanksgiving, Mayor Naftalin and I were having lunch at the café in the Grain Exchange building, where City Hall employees frequently went for lunch. Art had become mayor of Minneapolis in 1961, about a year after I was hired at the Urban League and while I was deeply involved with the fair housing endeavor. He was the first and only Jewish person to be elected as Minneapolis's mayor. Art was such a brilliant and caring mayor, and wanted to work with the NAACP and the Urban League in our civil rights and social justice work. I believe Alpha Smaby may have had something to do with my meeting him. Alpha knew of Art's background and his work with Hubert H. Humphrey, as well as his concerns about diversity and equality. My first meeting with Mayor Naftalin was very timely because that same year President Kennedy had established the Affirmative Action program.

Our brief walk to the restaurant had been pleasant. Winter hadn't set in yet, but we knew it was on its way. Snow would soon be falling, the winter winds would be howling, and the outdoor temperatures would be nearly unbearable. But that day the sun was shining and people were wearing light fall coats and jackets. I don't remember the focus of our meeting that day, but I will never forget what happened when we were almost finished with our lunch. One of the mayor's aides approached us and excused himself politely. "Pardon me, Mayor." I looked at the man and saw panic in his face. "The President has been shot," he said through tears. "It sounds serious."

The restaurant grew silent. I stood up and walked to the

window as if I might hear that a mistake had been made. "Come, Josie," said the mayor. The streets were unusually quiet as we hurried back to his office to confirm the terrible news. It was as though no one in Minneapolis could believe what had happened. I called Chuck and asked if he had heard, then I picked up my children from school. The drive home seemed slower than usual. The quiet desolation that took over the restaurant and the streets of downtown Minneapolis permeated the entire city.

At home, Chuck and I wept while we watched the news reports on television. We took turns calling our families and tried to explain to our children what had happened and why we were so devastated. Our daughters were too young to understand the depth of this loss to our people. They were not yet old enough to understand what Black people had endured for so long or why African Americans all over the country believed that Kennedy would be our champion. Based on the actions he had already taken in his brief tenure as the thirty-fifth President of the United States, we placed tremendous value on him and what we expected he would continue to accomplish on our behalf. Kennedy's assassination knocked the legs out from under us. We didn't know if his successor, Lyndon Johnson, would continue the work Kennedy had begun. We worried, too, about Jackie and their children. What would become of them?

7

BLACK WOMEN
IN THE STRUGGLE AND
WEDNESDAYS IN MISSISSIPPI

DOROTHY HEIGHT once said, "We must never lose sight of the quiet revolution that women are involved in. That, in the long run, will make all the difference." She was right.

One day near the beginning of the 1964 school year, Robert Williams called me into his office to tell me that he had received a call from Dr. Christiansen, the principal of Lincoln Junior High School in North Minneapolis. Christiansen was a keenly observant man who cared about his students, and he shared with us a pattern that was concerning him. His records showed that over a number of years the outcomes for Black girls who were high achieving when they entered eighth grade had decreased significantly by midyear. He thought it may have been due to the difficulty most students experience when transitioning from elementary school to junior high, but he did not want to risk taking that for granted. Because he wanted those students to succeed, he asked the Urban League for help.

I recruited a group of college-trained professional Black women—teachers, social workers, administrators, researchers—all mothers themselves. We met with Dr. Christiansen and after learning about and appreciating his long history with the students of Lincoln Junior High, we accepted the challenge to mentor the eight girls whom he had selected based in part on their elementary grades and behavior.

The women and I then met to discuss what our role would be in mentoring the girls. Like Dr. Christiansen, we too understood the difficulties inherent in the transition from elementary to junior high school. But in meeting with him, we also learned about something else: Black students who were not doing well often accused their peers who were achieving highly in school of "acting white." Not knowing the emphasis that Black people historically placed on education, some Black students associated academic success with being white. It was very possible that the eight girls were trying to avoid having to face that problem. If they didn't do well in school, they could be like the majority of students who were not acting white.

The natural African culture of caring for our students was and is very strong—holding children close, protecting them from any signs of harm, and telling them stories of their ancestors. We wanted those girls to learn about their history and their ancestral connection to education. We named our program the Junior Service League, and our goal was to keep the girls interested and motivated toward academic success, from then until they graduated high school, preparing them along the way for college acceptance. As mentors, we knew that the parents would have a strong influence on their daughters, so we invited them to meet and discuss our approach to mentoring the girls. Each mentor would meet with her mentee and her family and would develop a plan to attend events and programs. The parents were warm, accepting, and pleased with our plans.

Once we received parental permission, each Junior Service League member selected the young lady she would mentor. In addition, we agreed to meet with the girls' parents monthly to keep them apprised of what we were doing and to get their feedback. Our mothers also spent time with their families observing our method of interacting with their children, so they could approve of what we were doing. There was a feeling of familiarity reflective of African American culture in which people were used to family, relatives, and close friends helping in the development of children.

We all understood that the role of a mentor went beyond academic tutoring. The mentor models positive behavior. We understood that we were to be dependable, engaged in the needs of our student, and authentic. It was also critical that each mentee understood her role. She had to build trust in her mentor. She had to follow through on commitments we made to each other. She had to be open and honest and give us feedback on the goals we agreed to. It took time but we met our goals. Our students graduated.

The first summer of our program, President Lyndon Johnson enacted the Economic Opportunity Act of 1964, also known as the Federal War on Poverty. And in the following year, the Upward Bound program was launched as a part of that act. Stan Salett, a civil rights organizer, national education policy adviser, and one of the creators of the Head Start program, founded Upward Bound to provide low-income high school students with opportunities to prepare them for college.

I applied and the Junior Service League was accepted. Our girls were the first group of Black students to enroll in Upward Bound. Participants received instruction in literature, mathematics, and science on college campuses after school and on Saturdays, and during the summer at the University of St. Thomas in St. Paul. The program provided transportation to and from the colleges.

I was blessed with two mentees, Pamela Blackamoore and Cheryl Jones. Later, Cheryl's mother went back to college and completed her undergraduate degree and her social work degree, becoming an awarding-winning social worker in our community. Cheryl became an outstanding administrator in the Minneapolis public schools and a supporter of many community programs focused on young people. Her family was a part of one of the old Minneapolis families. Her uncle, Richard Green, became the Minneapolis School Superintendent in the 1980s.

Pamela became my family's fourth daughter. She spent weekends, holidays, and family events with us. My daughters loved her and treated her like family. We spent time in parks, looking at sunsets, and studying flowers and rocks. Pamela completed her college and advanced studies and became the director of the engineering and transportation department for the Minneapolis Public Schools.

I was thrilled when many years later, on March 18, 2008, several of the Upward Bound alumni gave me an award at Olson Junior High in North Minneapolis. My brother, Jim, was visiting from Houston and went with me. He was proud when he heard their tribute to me:

JOSIE JOHNSON

We honor you today for your humanitarian spirit,
your love for your people and mankind everywhere, your
determined spirit to uplift, and your dynamic smile.

Josie, you are exceptional in every way, unforgettable
to all who come in contact with you. We were blessed
and empowered by your mentoring of Lincoln Junior High's
little black girls with big dreams.

Pamela Blackamoore
Vicki Burrell
Cheryl Jones
Mardella Milton
Terryann Pettiford
Diane Westbrook

The afternoon ended with Cheryl Jones reading a lovely statement from her mother, Gladys Randle. Gladys was not only the mother of a Junior Service League member; she would also participate in other important efforts of ours in the coming years. From there, she went on to earn both a bachelor's degree in social work and a master's in social work from the University of Minnesota and eventually won several prestigious awards for her work in the field. In the statement Cheryl read, her mother praised me and my colleague Millie Roberts, saying, "I will always feel indebted to these two strong women who provided the courage and push I needed to complete my dreams."

By 1964, I had been a member of Delta Sigma Theta for fourteen years, having been initiated in 1950, the year before I graduated from Fisk. Delta Sigma Theta is the largest African American sorority and the fourth oldest, having been founded in 1913 at Howard University. Its mission and purpose are public service with a primary focus on the Black community.

Dorothy Height, who had been initiated in 1939 when I was nine years old, had been elected the sorority's president in 1951. Her history of civil rights work was already legendary when I entered Fisk, and she was a strong influence on my desperate desire to be accepted as a pledgee and become a Delta before graduating.

Until her death in 2010 at ninety-eight years of age, Dr. Height held many prestigious positions and was a formidable figure in political circles. She was the first Black staff member of the National YWCA and was president of the National Council of Negro Women (NCNW) for four decades. She followed the leadership and distinguished career of the great educator Mary McLeod Bethune, founder of Bethune-Cookman University, a historically Black college/university in Daytona, Florida. Dr. Bethune was appointed special adviser to President Franklin D. Roosevelt and was friends with the president and First Lady Eleanor Roosevelt. She also founded the NCNW in 1935. Like Dr. Bethune, Dorothy Height also served as a consultant to five U.S. presidents on the issue of civil rights and as such invited and accompanied Eleanor Roosevelt to a meeting of the council.

Dorothy was friends with people who were important to civil rights such as author/historian/sociologist W. E. B. Du Bois; the first Black Supreme Court Justice Thurgood Marshall, instrumental in the success of *Brown v. Board of Education*; journalist and publisher Daisy Bates, who played a major role in the Little Rock integration crisis of 1957; civil rights activist Fannie Lou Hamer, who cofounded the Mississippi Freedom Democratic Party; and Rosa Parks, known today as "the First Lady of civil rights" and "the mother of the freedom movement."

Dorothy also knew Dr. Kenneth Clark, author of the now-famous Doll Test, which he and his wife, Dr. Mamie Phipps Clark, devised in the 1940s to study the psychological effects of segregation on African American children. Drs. Clark used four dolls, identical except for color, to test children's racial perceptions. Their subjects, children between the ages of three and seven, were asked to identify both the race of the dolls and which color doll they preferred. A majority of the children preferred the white doll and assigned positive characteristics to it. The Clarks concluded that prejudice, discrimination, and segregation created a feeling of inferiority among African American children and damaged their self-esteem. Kenneth Clark was the first Black psychologist to earn a doctorate at Columbia University, to hold a permanent professorship at City College of New York, and to become president of the American Psychological Association. The doll test was part of his testimony in *Brown v. Board of Education*. In 2010, nearly two years after the election of Barack Obama, our first Black president—

and nearly seventy years after Drs. Clark devised the doll test—CNN commissioned renowned child psychologist and University of Chicago professor Margaret Beale Spencer, a leading researcher in the field of child development, to reinstitute it. Some would say that the Clarks would turn over in their graves if they saw that the results were the same as when they first developed it in the 1940s.

Dorothy Height was also among the women on the Lincoln Memorial stage with Martin Luther King Jr. when he delivered his iconic "I Have a Dream" speech at the March on Washington. And in 1967, she involved our sorority in a housing project that became known as the Sweat Equity Project. Following conversations with poor Black women in Mississippi, she along with Dorothy Dukes—the NCNW's housing expert—and Unita Blackwell, who would later become the first Black woman mayor in Mississippi, convinced officials at the Housing and Urban Development (HUD) department, the Office of Equal Opportunity (OEO), and a host of Mississippi housing experts to allow families who qualified for public housing to purchase HUD-held properties without a cash down payment. Instead, they were required to do $200 worth of maintenance work—sweat equity—as their down payment. The NCNW organized a homebuyers' association that trained members to repair, maintain, and occupy their homes for five years on a cooperative basis.

I was blessed to know Dr. Height well. I served with her on the National Board of Delta Sigma Theta and on the National Council of Negro Women when I became president of the Twin Cities Council in the early 1960s. She requested my involvement in many projects in which I was unable to participate because of time constraints. However, a call I received from her in the spring of 1964 was an invitation to participate in a project that I could not turn down. She told me that she and several of her peers (the leaders of other women's organizations—the National Women's Committee for Civil Rights, the National Council of Catholic Women, the National Council of Jewish Women, and United Church Women) had convened a three-day summit in Atlanta to address the treatment of women and girls who were jailed for their civil rights activities. She said that the women had heard firsthand accounts of brutalities inflicted on civil rights workers. And just as the session was about to end, Claire Harvey, the spokeswoman for the Jackson, Mississippi, group, issued a plea for northern women to visit regularly that summer and try to build bridges of communication between Jackson's Black and white communities.

She went on to tell me that she and her dear friend, Polly Cowan, of the National Council of Jewish Women, had decided to answer the call. They had heard that there was a lot of abuse of women and girls in their efforts to register and vote. They were organizing a project that they were calling Wednesdays in Mississippi. Every week that summer, small teams of Black and white women from Northern cities would travel to Mississippi in an effort to reach across the chasms of race, class, geography, and religion to help end segregation in America.

In the summer of 1964, there were many voter registration efforts taking place in the South. The Congress on Racial Equality (CORE), the Student Non-Violent Coordinating Committee (SNCC), and the Council of Federated Organizations (COFO) were planning the Mississippi Project, also known as Freedom Summer, a voter registration project. Approximately one hundred white college students had helped COFO register voters in November 1963, and now several hundred more Black and white students were invited back for Freedom Summer. SNCC organizer Robert Moses had made a call for white Ivy League students to volunteer, and Polly Cowan thought this would be a perfect time for Northern women from what she called the "Cadillac crowd"—

women of stature, both Black and white, of various faiths and interests, who appeared beyond reproach—to follow suit. Every week in June and July 1964, a new group of women would go to Mississippi from Tuesday through Thursday.

I was deeply honored by Dorothy's invitation to participate in this—the only civil rights project organized by and for women. Wednesdays in Mississippi would be a project that would consist of seven interracial and interfaith teams of five to seven women tasked with secretly bringing supplies and much-needed support to small rural Mississippi communities where local Black citizens and Black and white civil rights workers from the North were facing daily violence and constant harassment as they worked side by side to end legalized segregation. Because the attorney general ordered that we couldn't talk about the project to others, it would later be classified as a "quiet project" of courage, danger, and transformation.

Chuck and I had a lengthy discussion about the wisdom of accepting Dorothy's invitation and going on this trip. He had been incredibly patient and supportive of my many late-night meetings, our late dinners, and so many other inconveniences. But there were very real dangers associated with voter registration in the South, and in particular in Mississippi. Civil rights workers faced constant abuse and harassment from Mississippi's white population. The KKK, police, and even state and local authorities carried out a systematic series of violent attacks including arson, beatings, false arrests, and murder. Three young college student activists, James Chaney, Andrew Goodman, and Michael Schwerner, had recently gone missing and were feared dead, which caused some of the white Northerners who had been interested in Wednesdays in Mississippi to change their minds. Chuck and I had three little girls ages ten, eight, and six. We had to consider how he would care for them if I was jailed or badly injured, or worse, if I did not return. Was it worth it? We decided that the opportunity to be a part of such a creative and new effort to help the civil rights cause and to gather information about the struggle and courage of Black citizens in Mississippi was worth the risks. So we decided to have faith that the group would be protected and that I would return to him and our children safe and sound.

Polly Cowan became the director of the project and the National Council of Negro Women backed it financially. She organized volunteers with the help of the League of Women Voters and the American Association of University Women. An impressive group of women were recruited to go, including the wife of the governor of New Jersey and the wife of the president of Massachusetts Institute of Technology. The Minneapolis team was identified as Team 4 and was composed of two Black women, myself and Mary Kyle, publisher of the *Twin Cities Courier,* and two white women, Maxine Nathanson of the National Council of Jewish Women, and Barbara Cunningham, chair of the Brooklyn Center Human Relations Committee.

I was very impressed with the way the project was organized: every detail was meticulously coordinated, including travel and safety precautions, how we would interact with one another while in Mississippi, and how we would dress. Many of the women had never been to the South. For them, this would be a lesson in the Southern way of life. For instance, the Black and white women could not be seen speaking to each other publicly and could not lodge together. We were told of police traps such as handmade stop signs or extremely low speed limits. And so that we wouldn't stand out, we were advised to dress like the women of the South. The white women were advised to wear white gloves and we Black women were advised to dress in the manner of the people we were relating to so as to meld into the Black community. It was Dorothy's contention, and rightly so, that "we could not bring about change if we went down there and tried to upset it." We all had to agree to use our own specific talents to help the Black residents of Mississippi and commit to work on civil rights in our own communities once we returned to them.

Virginia Bourne, vice president of the Southern region of the YWCA, came to Minneapolis to give us a thorough orientation. We would fly to Chicago together and then have to separate and not be allowed to speak to one another in public again until we returned home, for fear that our Northern accents could cause us harm. In fact, we were forbidden to speak aloud in public at all, for the same reason. Chuck and I had been away from our home state of Texas for nearly ten years and had acquired enough of a Northern accent that it could have been detected by a listening ear, so I knew it was important to comply. In addition, we were given strict instructions by Attorney General Robert Kennedy, the brother of our late president, that because we were helping to effect massive change in an environment known for horrific violence against Black people and civil rights workers, we must tell no one that we were going except his office and our immediate families.

The Minneapolis team was scheduled to go to Mississippi on July 28–30 in 1964. We would fly into Jackson on Tuesday, visit a freedom school in Vicksburg on Wednesday, and return home on Thursday. My poor little girls' tears on the day I left were heart wrenching. Chuck and I had been candid with our children. They knew where I was going and why, and they knew of the danger, even the possibility that they may not see their mother again. Yet we all knew that I had to do this, though they may not have understood fully because of their young ages.

Our team met at the Minneapolis airport and flew to Chicago. When we reached Chicago, Virginia made sure that the two Black women and the two white women would be separated for the remainder of the trip. Our four team members had bonded over the months of planning, and it was very difficult for us to suddenly have to act like we didn't know each other. Maxine was particularly shocked and upset when we were told to separate. We'd had two orientations, but she missed the one where this information was shared, and unfortunately none of us had remembered to tell her.

We couldn't help being a little afraid. We didn't know what we were going to face in Mississippi. But there were times when I had to ask myself why I was so scared. I grew up in the segregated South, in Houston, where my family and I were denied the right to drink from certain water fountains, dine in certain restaurants, and were relegated to use the "colored" restrooms when we were out in public. But Mississippi was different—it presented far more danger than I had ever felt in Texas. I felt more afraid in Mississippi, very unsafe. I didn't know how our people survived the attitude and behavior I was seeing and feeling.

When our plane landed in Jackson, Maxine and Barbara were greeted by their host family and immediately whisked off, leaving Mary and me standing there waiting for our host family, who was late. I was unnerved, convinced that the Klan had done something evil to them and was lying in wait for us. I looked around the airport, frantically imagining Klansmen everywhere and trying to identify which of the people moving around the airport might be KKK, sure that they would not wear their white robes and hoods in such a public place. The ten minutes Mary and I had to wait for our host family seemed like hours. We were so relieved when they arrived. It turned out that the wife, who was a teacher, had been delayed at a meeting she had to attend at her school. Later, Maxine would tell us that she was taken aback when she and Barbara entered their family's home. The hostess rushed to close the drapes in her fine home in a well-kept neighborhood, fearing that her neighbors would see strange guests and cause harm to her family.

The activities of our two teams on Tuesday were very different. Maxine and Barbara met with local ladies in one of their living rooms over tea and cookies. The Southern white women openly discussed their fears and suspicions about the civil rights movement and many, for the first time, voiced their support for change. At that time in Mississippi, mixing with outsiders had dire consequences, yet the women came and listened, and their hearts and minds began to open. Those clandestine meetings became the catalyst for great change.

When Mary and I left the airport, our hosts took us to a meeting in a Black Baptist church where people were receiving orientation and instruction on voter registration activities. When we drove up to the church, I was surprised to see two men with shotguns guarding the church during the meeting. I noticed that they took turns: one would walk around the perimeter of the church while the other stood guard. Inside, we were greeted warmly and learned much about the procedures that were being used to help Black citizens get registered to vote. At the end of the meeting we were taken to a café. I couldn't help cringing when the owner, a kindly, concerned man, warned us to watch our every step.

We were then taken to our host family's home to settle in and sleep. Before going to bed, our wonderful host invited us into her living room where we had a serious and deep conversation. Hearing her share her experiences of living in Jackson during that volatile time coupled with seeing the courage of the people at the church helped us settle in to prepare for the activities that would take place on Wednesday. Both the white and Black host families were instructed to give us another briefing on our trip and a packet that contained our itinerary, schedules, a copy of *The Northside Reporter* (a weekly newspaper published in Jackson and edited by Pulitzer Prize–winner Hazel Brannon Smith), a pamphlet on the Mississippi Freedom Democratic Party, *The Student Voice* (published weekly in Atlanta), a sheet explaining the

Mississippi Summer Project, a two-page piece on incidents that had taken place in Mississippi on July 17–20, and another pamphlet distributed by the Citizens Council. I believe each team was given updated incident reports for the week they were there.

Wednesday was the day the quiet revolution took place. The day was packed with activities, beginning with a visit to Jackson State University, a historically black university, where we met with teachers-in-training. The teachers told us that Negro schools were given outdated and dilapidated books that had been passed down after white students finished with them. Some of the books were filled with brainwashing information that espoused segregation, such as "God did not intend for people to be equal or integrated. He made black birds, red birds, robins, etc., and you never see them mixing." They told us that the children in both Black and white schools were brainwashed from the cradle throughout their educational experiences. We were saddened to learn that Black students were discouraged from affiliating with the movement, told that it would interfere with their education.

Immediately following our time at Jackson State, the four members of our team met at a hotel where we were given the supplies we would take to the freedom school in Vicksburg and were picked up by the friendly young Black man who would drive us there. Once we were in the car heading for the highway, he told us the drive would be about forty-five minutes. Under other circumstances, we would have enjoyed a relaxing drive, but there we were, two Black women and two white women in a car being driven by a Black man, with a car full of white people following close behind quietly but threateningly, trying to intimidate us by their presence. We knew that anything could happen in the time it would take to get to the freedom school. It was the longest forty-five minutes I have ever spent.

As we drove along, the stunning beauty of the landscape surprised me. Mississippi is a beautiful state. The countryside is full of lush green grass and fragrant magnolia, cypress, and evergreen trees under an endless sky. It was a beauty marred by the state's terrible history of Klansmen burning crosses in front of the homes of my people, sometimes burning their houses down because of perceived or made-up crimes, a beauty marred by lynchings echoed in the lyrics of "Strange Fruit," the song made famous by Billie Holiday: "Southern trees bear strange fruit / Blood on the leaves and blood at the root / Black bodies swinging in the southern breeze / Strange fruit hanging from the poplar trees." It was hard to reconcile that beauty with the evil and ugliness, the horrible abuse of people that was going on down there. As in our Twin Cities, the Mississippi River flows along Vicksburg. Down there, though, it is as wide as the ocean. As we drove over the marshlands stretching out on both sides of the highway, I couldn't help wondering if the bodies of the missing civil rights volunteers James Chaney, Andrew Goodman, and Michael Schwerner might be found there.

The organized freedom schools were established in 1964 during Freedom Summer. By then it was undeniable that the *Brown v. Board of Education* ruling wasn't working, as the South continued its pattern of segregation. Mississippi closed all of its public schools and white children were sent to "academies." Black children had no place left to learn. The freedom schools were intended to be temporary alternative schools for Black elementary through high school students to achieve social, political, and economic equality. Volunteer teachers taught them. Some of the schools were held in parks, kitchens, residential homes, or outside under trees, but most were held in churches or church basements. We had been told that the freedom school in Vicksburg was one of the worst, if not the worst, in Mississippi. When we arrived, I saw why. The school was in a dilapidated old house in an isolated area high on a hill. A widow named Mrs. Brown lived there with her eight children. Behind the house was a barn that had been converted to a library, where we observed college students sorting boxes of books sent from the North and placing them on newly configured library shelves. Those Black and white college students served as both teachers and librarians. When we toured the school and talked with the children and the teacher/librarians, we witnessed the hope and promise of change that was engendered there even as we experienced firsthand the devastating results of racial injustice. We were saddened to learn from our host family and again from the workers at the freedom school that there was a hush in the Black community. People in certain positions were afraid of losing their jobs. Further, they feared worse things could be done to them, so they tended to be very guarded, unsure of how much they could say.

When we left the school, our driver took us to see Vicksburg's Black community. First we drove through a relatively nice district with homes that appeared secure. But then, just one block later, we went through a community of poorly constructed, weather-beaten row houses and shacks built on stilts, some without windows, others with broken windows. I was immediately reminded of the houses near my childhood home on Rusk Street in Houston—a community with poorly designed, shotgun-style houses like the ones I saw here in Mississippi. My heart broke as I remembered the fire that destroyed the Mills family's home, and I wondered if there were any families in the nicer neighborhood who, like my parents, would take in families left homeless if there were to be a fire. Yet I was also struck by the friendliness of the people who lived in those ramshackle homes. Many were sitting on the steps of those old houses and waved as we drove by. There is one woman whose image is still with me to this day. We had stopped to get a closer view of the area that our driver said was patterned after the plantations from slavery times. The woman was thin and was wearing a tattered blue work dress. And she looked tired, since she had probably been working all day. Yet she was so pleasant to us, bearing out the Southern way of showing kindness to strangers.

Before leaving Vicksburg, we attended an underground meeting at St. Mary's Roman Catholic Church, where an interfaith group of priests, pastors, and rabbis were meeting together: Father John Kist, the church's priest; a Methodist clergy; two Episcopal clergymen; a rabbi; a young married woman; a young couple; and a COFO student named John Ferguson. Except for Mary and me, the group was all white. We learned that those clerics wanted to do something but felt as though their hands were tied. They told us that attempts had been made throughout the state of Mississippi to get interracial groups together to discuss the problem, but there was one stumbling block after another. They were reluctant to speak out to their congregations, unsure of which, if any, of their members were KKK or police who were supposed to enforce the law but refused to do so, reporting them to the authorities if they spoke favorably about voter registration.

Following the meeting, we returned to Jackson. We quickly ate box lunches at the YWCA and then were rushed to the Federal Court House for a hearing of the State Advisory Committee to the Civil Rights Commission, where we would hear Black people testify to a judge about ill treatment they had received from police and employers. We were about an hour late because our morning activities in Vicksburg were of such great interest that it was hard to break away. We were told that only a few people agreed to sit on the committee, which was composed of four Blacks and five whites who had volunteered to counsel the people who were testifying on the most effective ways to ensure that they would be heard.

We sat in the back of the courtroom and listened as adults and children testified about treatment they had suffered at the hands of police officers. We heard story after story of false arrests and of people losing their jobs because they had gone to a voter rights meeting. Horrible stories. Mother after mother pleaded with the judge to release their children from jail, mostly teenage boys, who had been beaten by policemen and arrested for no reason; we heard from fathers and teachers who had been fired from their jobs, and from people telling of their cars being set on fire. Except for one young COFO boy, everyone who presented evidence was Black.

Maxine said she could not believe that the horrible incidents we heard in the courtroom that day could happen in America. The treatment described was worse than the way animals were treated, and protection was completely absent. Mary and I, the two Blacks on our team, were unfortunately not surprised. We were all too aware of the crimes committed by people and agencies enlisted to protect and to serve. Nor were we surprised to hear that laws were often made up at the time a so-called crime was committed. However, we were all dismayed that no matter how much the people who testified cried and pleaded, the judge was unmoved. He did not release anyone from jail; he showed no mercy whatsoever.

Wednesday night ended with a delightful dinner at Tougaloo College with the president, Dr. Adam Beittel, his wife, and faculty members. Dinner was served by students, who spoke of Tougaloo as the "oasis of the South." It was such a wonderful climax for our Minnesota team's trip to Mississippi. After dinner, Dr. Beittel essentially confirmed all that we had seen and experienced in the two days we were there. However, hearing it from a man of his stature reassured us, at least the two white members of our team, that the conditions we saw were not simply a way to sell newspapers. In addition, he helped us to better understand that the fear of white citizens who felt the need for change was not being dramatized to attract attention: it was very real.

We left early Thursday morning, boarding the plane separately, with the good wishes of Virginia Bourne, who had come to Minneapolis to train us. But when we arrived back in Minneapolis, we received devastating news: the Vicksburg freedom school we visited had been bombed Wednesday night. Thankfully no one was at the school at the time, but I was crushed with feelings of guilt, wondering if it was our fault. Maybe it wouldn't have happened if we had stayed home or not visited the school.

I didn't have much time to stay immersed in those guilty feelings. It was back to family life. Chuck and the girls couldn't stop hugging me, they were so relieved that I returned home safely. And the team had much more work to do. Part of our commission was that all the members of each of the seven Wednesdays in Mississippi teams from across the country were to work on civil rights in their respective communities once they returned home. The idea was to persuade Congress to act on the need for voter rights, voter registration, and the protection of our people.

Participating in Wednesdays in Mississippi and witnessing what we saw and heard in Jackson had a lasting effect on me. It showed me just how mean people can be—the human-to-human level of meanness. It made me aware of the depths of the teachings of white supremacy and racism, and the legacy of the teaching of slave owners who justified their treatment of our ancestors and created laws to support that teaching. I have concluded that although the struggle takes on different forms and requires different strategies, the basic struggle is the same.

The Wednesdays in Mississippi quiet revolution worked. It contributed greatly to the passing of the Voting Rights Act by President Johnson on August 6, 1965, and enacted by the 89th Congress. We were only then allowed to talk more freely about our experience. However, only Maxine

Nathanson and I were able by then—Mary Kyle had passed away, and we had lost contact with Barbara Cunningham. Maxine and I were invited to talk about Wednesdays in Mississippi in Twin Cities Black communities, and we received invitations to speak in suburban communities as well.

Once our trip was made public through newspaper articles, Maxine and her husband received several very frightening anti-Semitic phone calls. Her husband thought they should ignore the calls, but after having seen firsthand the evil that racist and anti-Semitic individuals are capable of, Maxine believed they needed to take those calls very seriously. But that didn't stop her from continuing with the work.

I am so excited that there has been a renewed interest in Wednesdays in Mississippi. In 2011, I was invited by a young Black filmmaker, Marlene McCurtis, to participate in a panel discussion in Memphis. She has been developing a documentary about the program and arranged several appearances and presentations with the program's participants. There we were, presented in a public forum in a beautiful new library, to the city of Memphis, along with the Little Rock Nine and their surviving Central High classmates. At the time of this writing, Marlene McCurtis is still working on the film, and we all hope she will be able to raise enough funds to complete it.

In June 2014, during the fiftieth anniversary of Freedom Summer, an intergenerational conference was held in Jackson to commemorate it and to continue the encouragement of our youth. I participated in a panel discussion about Wednesdays in Mississippi, along with women who served on teams from several other communities and staff member Susan Goodwillie. Also in 2014, Debbie Harwell published a book, *Wednesdays in Mississippi: Proper Ladies Working for Radical Change, Freedom Summer 1964*. The book had begun as her dissertation, and she invited me and other Wednesday in Mississippi participants to an event in my hometown at the University of Houston for an event to celebrate its publication.

• • •

In 1965, the Office of Economic Development created an experimental project that brought Twin Cities private agency social workers and the federal government together in a partnership to assist parents in low-income communities in developing better parenting skills. Called Project ENABLE (Education and Neighborhood Action for Better Living Environment), it was the first project in the nation to bring a federal government agency together with private social service agencies to share their practices and knowledge of working with communities in order to support the strengthening of family life in a disadvantaged community.

The project established partnerships among the Urban League, the Jewish Family Children's Service, the Minneapolis Family and Children's Service, and the federal government. I was the director of the Minneapolis project, assisted by my colleague Millie Roberts, a seasoned social worker who worked with the Minneapolis Family and Children's Service. Willie Mae Wilson, president of the St. Paul Urban League, directed the project in St. Paul.

The objective of Project ENABLE was to help poor parents identify their most troubling parenting issues and to engage existing community resources to help them improve their child rearing practices. We developed a list of respected individuals in each community. We shared contacts and began having neighborhood discussion groups, working together to plan the methods we would use to engage with and help our families to share their concerns. The concerns turned out to be more than child rearing issues: they were also about the effects of poverty and racism on both parents and children.

A curriculum evolved from the discussions. We began training professional staff on effective ways of listening to parents, which proved helpful in addressing their concerns. During this phase, we were able to help some of our parents recognize the connection between negative responses

86

to their children's behavior and their fear for their children's safety and well-being. For Black parents, this fear originated in slavery when there was an urgency to protect children from the very real threats their actions could have on their lives. Too often our parents believe that they need to employ harsh parenting tactics in order to help their children, especially boys. Our task was to help parents understand this negative association and to teach them ways to begin responding differently.

I recall one day when I was walking down a busy street with a Minneapolis ENABLE parent and her child. The child moved too close to the street and the mother grabbed him, screamed at him, and called him unflattering names. I took the opportunity to talk with the mother about her reaction and helped her think about the effect her screaming and name-calling could have on him. I then showed her a better way that such an incident could be handled in the future. There were many such examples, and fortunately our parents welcomed the discussions about more positive parental reactions.

The Project ENABLE team believed there was much value in the teamwork and information sharing we engaged in, and the recruitment of helpers from the neighborhoods was very effective in helping us develop an appreciation of untapped resources. Working with people who are known and respected in their communities was ultimately very helpful in accomplishing our mission.

Unfortunately, there was only a two-year budget, and the funding was not renewed. This was frustrating because two years was not enough time for us to model the methodology and value of methods we were testing. However, some of the agencies, including the Minneapolis Urban League, continued with the model. As with so many initiatives in Black communities, I have often wondered what would have happened if the program or a facsimile of it had been funded

My mother, Josie Bell McCullough Robinson,
in 1929, the year she and my father were married.

In the arms of my father, Judson Wilbur Robinson Sr., 1930.

With Mother and Father when I am a few months old.

With my Aunt Josie
in her yard in
Houston, 1931.

My paternal grandparents, Willie Robinson
and Henry Columbus Robinson.

Around five years old,
in Houston.

My Grandmother Mommie and Grandfather A.K.,
seated at center in their drugstore in San Antonio,
Leonard's on the West Side, where I worked in the summers.

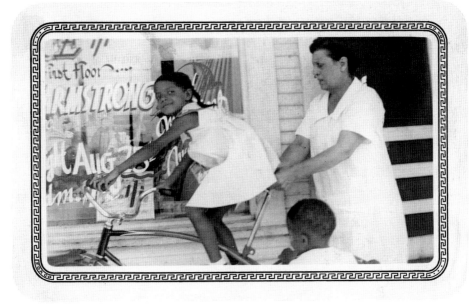

On a delivery bike in front of the drugstore with Mommie and brother Judson.

With Father at our
Nagle Street home in
Houston, late 1930s.

In the backyard at Nagle Street in Houston in the late 1940s. Left to right: my brother Judson Jr., Mother, Father, me, and my brother James.

My freshman year photo at Fisk University in 1947.

I was crowned Miss Fisk at Fisk Chapel in 1950 by the president of Fisk University, Dr. Charles A. Johnson.

Charles and I married on June 27, 1951. My parents are on the left and Charles's mother, Hattie, is on the right.

My beloved daughters, from left: Josie Irene, Patrice Yvonne, and Norrene Elaine.

Holding the Minnesota delegation sign from the March
on Washington in Washington, D.C., in 1963, with two other
delegates from Minnesota, including my friend Zetta Feder (right).
Photograph by Marty Nordstrom; reprinted with permission.

At the airport following our
participation in the "quiet
program" known as Wednesdays
in Mississippi, in 1964. Maxine
Nathanson is at left, and Mary
Kyle is at right. Photograph by Donald
Black. Copyright 1964 Star Tribune.

With family members of our Project ENABLE program in downtown Minneapolis, 1967. I am second from the right.

Listening to University of Minnesota students in the late 1960s.

The first Black person on the University of Minnesota
Board of Regents, 1971. Photograph by John Croft. Copyright 1973 Star Tribune.

Speaking at an antiwar rally at Coffman Union
at the University of Minnesota on January 19, 1973.
Photograph by John Croft. Copyright 1973 Star Tribune.

With Elmer Andersen.
Courtesy of University Archives,
University of Minnesota Libraries.

My family, circa 1975.
Left to right: Josie Irene,
Chuck, Norrene Elaine,
myself, and Patrice Yvonne.

My daughter Patrice during her internship for Vice President
Walter Mondale when she was a graduate student.

At the age of fifty-five (with my first grandchild), celebrating
my graduation and my doctorate degree from Amherst in 1986.

Lorenzo "Pete" Williams and I on his boat,
during one of our many wonderful trips together.

With Dr. Dorothy Height, my mentor and inspiration
in the women's struggle for justice, at a meeting of
the National Council of Negro Women, circa 1998.

With my dear friend Mahmoud El-Kati at the Saint Paul Hotel in 2013.

Longtime friend and ally Walter "Fritz" Mondale.
Photograph by Anthony Souffle. Copyright 2018 Star Tribune.

With President Obama on June 1, 2012, in Minnesota.

My dear daughters,
Josie Irene and
Norrene Elaine.

My lovely granddaughters, from left: Lauren Noelle, Josie Helen, and Rosa Patrice.

My beautiful great-grandchildren, from left: Lucy Josephine, Niko Stephen Eugene, and Ella May.

so that we could have continued with proper staffing and resources.

The parents and community enjoyed their time together. At the end of the program, the members of the Minneapolis ENABLE Mothers' Club spent time creating a book of recipes, which one of the mothers requested so she could vary her family menus. The book was a gift each member gave one another at the end of the project. It also served as a reminder of our group.

Millie Roberts reported her observations about the impact she believed the project made on her work. As I have thought more about the possibilities of Project ENABLE—a program funded for listening to parents, appreciating the deep fear most Black parents had about the safety of their children, engaging social workers mindful of the public view of African American people, and collaborative methods to improve parenting skills—I felt that it could have responded to community and family needs in meaningful ways in the mid-1960s, when Black families were experiencing various forms of personal and collective stress.

The National Urban League is credited with developing the first organized social work course of study for African Americans at Fisk University. The influences of African American sociologist and first Black president of Fisk, Dr. Charles S. Johnson, as well as the research of Fisk graduate W.E.B. Du Bois on social services within the African American communities, caused me to switch my college major from medicine to sociology. If Project ENABLE had continued, I may have been able to continue employing my specialization, responding to family and community needs in productive ways.

Today, we Black people are once again talking about "saving our children." We are returning to the trust in pioneer social workers such as Iris Carlton-LaNey and other African American social workers who are working as a collective group. We were aware of the early history written in 1898–1916 by those early social workers. They lived in the Black community, and as African Americans themselves, they shared many of the issues that affected their clients. They were determined to link the needs of the families they worked with to the resources they saw and felt would help. They were also aware of race issues—the historical experiences the community faced. The issues of self-help, understanding their behavior, and race pride were important to Black pioneers of social work practice.

8

MAKING OUR WAY

BY THE MID-1960S, cities across the nation were in turmoil, reacting to the events of the decade. We had accomplished the passage of the Civil Rights Act, the Voting Rights Act, and the Fair Housing Act, but those victories were not without severe repercussions. Jobs were still scarce, and civil rights workers were still being harassed and murdered for their efforts to help Blacks in the South to register to vote. Stokely Carmichael had become chair of the Student Nonviolent Coordinating Committee, and its members were losing faith in the strategy of nonviolence. The Black Panther Party had become organized and was offering a different method in the struggle for justice.

Here in Minneapolis, things were also changing. The Phyllis Wheatley Settlement House, which had once been a major gathering place on the North Side, was becoming less important to some in the community. Since the 1920s, Wheatley House had provided a variety of programs for our children including after-school programs and piano and dance lessons. Training for young men who boxed with the Golden Gloves was offered under the direction of W. Harry Davis, who would later become a leading Minneapolis civil rights activist, businessman, and mayoral candidate. He and his wife and children had become dear friends of ours. Wheatley

House had also been the social center for Black college students, who, unwelcome in University of Minnesota dormitories, were given lodging. Fraternity and sorority dances and basketball tournaments were held there as well as dances and plays for neighborhood youth and families. Wheatley also provided rehearsal space and lodging for famous artists and musicians such as Duke Ellington and Billie Holiday because Minneapolis hotels refused to accommodate them when they performed here.

North Minneapolis was a close-knit community before the problems of the '60s broke out. Just like the families of my childhood in Houston, North Side families knew and looked out for one another. Neighbors knew the names of the children, whether they lived in the projects or in modest or middle-to-upper-class homes. North Minneapolis was diverse. African American, Jewish, Mexican, Native American, and white families lived on the Near North Side but were segregated in specific areas around Sumner Field, the center of the community located behind Wheatley House. Children from all the groups that made up the community played together, even though parents, especially the white parents, often did not approve.

Black-owned businesses like barber shops and beauty salons, restaurants, bars and cafés, dry cleaners, grocery stores, and clothing stores thrived. The Givens Ice Cream Bar was also a mainstay of the community, owned by Archie Givens Sr. and his wife, Phebe. Archie and Phebe grew up in North Minneapolis and remained there with their children while he grew his career as a real estate developer building new homes for Black families. He would later become known for integrating nursing homes in and around the Twin Cities and later, along with Phebe, for establishing the Givens Foundation for African American Literature. The Givenses were one of the families who welcomed Chuck and me to the Twin Cities in 1956.

In the late 1950s and early 1960s, urban renewal policies and white flight to the suburbs destroyed stable and historic Black communities in North and South Minneapolis and Saint Paul with the construction of I-94 and 35W highways. Homes were torn down, and the promises made to residents that new housing would be built were not kept. The majority of Black businesses were forced to close. Families who could afford to move relocated to other communities. As a result, the neighborhoods have never fully recovered.

Even following passage of the 1955 Minnesota State Act for Fair Employment Practices, a majority of employed Blacks in the Twin Cities still held only menial or service jobs, and most believed that the cause had more to do with racism and white supremacy than lack of education. North Side residents argued that there was little opportunity available to them and that equality had only been achieved on paper, not in reality. In addition, most of the businesses on Plymouth Avenue, the major business hub in North Minneapolis, were now Jewish-owned rather than being owned by Black residents, who had stayed after Jewish people moved out of the neighborhood. Blacks felt a lack of control over the economy in their own neighborhood. This eventually led to confrontation between Blacks and Jewish business owners, which came in the form of two rebellions, characterized by mainstream media as "riots"—one in 1966 and the other in 1967. Those events were not simply random acts of violence. Residents were striking back at the origin of violence: oppression.

Shortly after our return from the March on Washington back in 1963, Mayor Naftalin had publicly asserted his belief that there was a need to enforce equality in the city. In his 1963 inaugural speech for his reelection to a third term as mayor of Minneapolis, he predicted that "a fire of protest against indignity and denial is burning here as it is elsewhere. It will not be extinguished by promises or pledges that are not translated into action." Also in that year, he made a request to Robert Williams that I be granted a leave of absence from the Urban League to serve as an adviser to him. For the next few years, we continued working on jobs, education, and housing here in Minneapolis. Mayor Naftalin was the first Minneapolis mayor to actually visit the North Side and have meaningful conversations with community members.

After the rebellions broke out in 1966 and 1967, the mayor's office and I worked with North Minneapolis citizens to find ways to resolve the problems that had been identified. We worked very quickly to make several important resolutions: to provide jobs for young people and to bring together a coalition of leaders from the Black and Jewish communities. Those meetings resulted in the formation of the Commission on Human Development. The commission, composed of public officials, was given a year to complete the tasks of determining the causes of the recent violence and making recommendations to prevent its recurrence.

I remember, with a sense of accomplishment, a very good discussion and understanding by the mayor of a strategy I thought was different—and had the possibility of being more effective than those previously tried in the struggle for civil rights. I had created a spreadsheet on the wall of the mayor's office that (1) identified all the programs that had been offered over time to achieve civil rights; (2) spelled out the objectives and mission we wanted to accomplish; (3) identified what needed to be done to achieve our goals; and (4) identified the roadblocks to the goals. Our public report would include our findings, resources needed, financial support, legislation, personnel, time, and so on. We studied it and began considering how and with whom to discuss this new process both locally and nationally.

• • •

When the rebellions broke out, the staff at the Urban League and an ad hoc group of community members were aptly prepared to work on the challenges identified by the Black community. A new organization, The Way Opportunities Unlimited, Inc., was formed with a focus on education and service to Black youth on the North Side. Phyllis Wheatley House was still important to the community, but it was a settlement house, and the generation that was coming of age in the 1960s was confronted with discrimination and prejudice on a level they hadn't experienced before. According to Spike Moss, "At Wheatley, all that was required was for us to have fun. Now we needed something to fit today's thing—it couldn't fit yesterday." The Way was the organization designed and managed to address the issues of the day.

An impressive and significant cross-section of Minneapolis communities came together to support The Way. Well-known public leaders in the legal, financial, cultural, and religious communities were able to see the value of this new agency, and confirmed its value by offering financial and legal support as well as much needed moral support. I participated as a supporter, representing the Urban League, the mayor's Office, and other outreach connections with whom I had associations.

The Way was a voice heard throughout the community. Its mission included strengthening family life, protecting African American children, and developing pride in the history of our people in America. One of the programs Mahmoud El-Kati developed through The Way was a Black history class for inmates at Stillwater Prison. I worked with the education team to develop the curriculum and was one of the instructors who visited the facility once a month with the education team where we taught the inmates—men who were enthusiastic about learning their history. We also worked with Antioch University in Yellow Springs, Ohio, to develop a campus here that was connected with The Way.

As the Minneapolis Urban League's community organizer, I was accepted and welcomed and began to participate in many of The Way's activities and programs. I was involved in meetings with community members, and Chuck and I were very much engaged in the development of this positive endeavor, often taking our daughters with us to meetings and other activities. I recall a particular meeting in the basement of The Way, where community activists and those associated with the organization determined that the Black community should form an independent nation; we discussed taking this plan to the United Nations. Chuck, always a practical voice in discussions, asked about some specific requirements for a nation. "Did we have a military, a national budget, or a governmental structure that would support the needs of citizens?" he asked. We did not, and as a result the idea to secede from the United States was not raised again within our group.

I developed close relationships with The Way's cofounders, Syl and Gwen Davis; Verlena Matey-Keke, coordinator of the education department; Vusumuzi Zulu, editor of the organization's newsletter; youth leader Spike Moss; and Mahmoud El-Kati, director of the education department, who would become a lifelong friend. He recently told me when recalling The Way: "Let it be said that The Way Opportunities Unlimited, Inc., was part and parcel of the spirit of awareness and the movement of ideas to address long-standing inequities, which seem to ebb and flow with the ideals of a democratic American society."

The Way became a center for information on the National Black Liberation Movement and was embraced by young activists who saw it as a source of Black pride and engagement in community. The Way represented a source of Black Power, self-determination, and hope. In addition, it became a must-stop visit on their travel agenda for some of the nation's most prominent Black figures, including soul singer James Brown, boxer Muhammad Ali, and Cleveland

Mayor Carl Stokes. Just like my father when he came to visit, people would ask where the Black community was. They were led to The Way.

The Way closed in 1970 as a result of financial struggles and increased competition for resources within the Black community. Ironically, a police station was built on The Way's historical and once-hopeful location. But the community has not forgotten it. In fact, when a young Black man named Jamar Clark was killed by police in November 2015, one of the demands made by the protestors from Black Lives Matter was that The Way be reinstated, to its original site.

On August 6, 2016, The Way celebrated its fiftieth anniversary of its founding. At the event, my dear friend Rolland Robinson, a white man who is a retired minister of Calvary Methodist Church, and was president of The Way's board, released his book *For a Moment We Had The Way*. It is a wonderful book of his reflections on the organization, which he begins by saying, "Older souls, no matter their age, have made my soul wiser, spoke of what we thought, told us of what we knew, that gave us each leave to be what we are, truly."

9

TEACHING OUR HISTORY

THE DAY MARTIN LUTHER KING WAS ASSASSINATED was terrible for people all over the country. There was shock and mourning throughout the nation—including Minneapolis. Dr. King, who worked so hard to end violence, had died in such a violent manner and there was confusion everywhere. In North Minneapolis, tears were rampant and cries of "They killed our King, they killed our King" were heard throughout the community. Emotions were already high due to an incident during which police had attacked a young Black woman at the Aquatennial Parade several weeks before. I think Dr. King's assassination sent the community over the edge. Unable to think of rational ways to express their grief, young people began throwing bricks and setting businesses on fire. The police and fire departments were unable to quell this disturbance and the National Guard was called in.

Chuck and I, with our daughters, rushed to Plymouth Avenue. Once there, we saw children in the streets who seemed lost and confused. We gathered them up and took them to The Way, where we knew they would be safe. Concerned about our safety, our friends discouraged our involvement. But community engagement was so ingrained in us that safety concerns were simply not an issue. Being of assistance in the effort to strengthen the North Side community far overrode those concerns.

The people I was involved with—my friends at The Way, as well as Mayor Naftalin and others who were deeply involved in civil rights—wanted very much to connect with people in the South. We wanted them to know that we here in Minnesota were mourning our tragic loss as much as people in the South and in the larger cities in the North. We began organizing community meetings, reflecting some of the same strategies and sharing outcomes with friends we knew in other communities who were outstanding, well-known activists. We shared what we had learned from strategists such as Anna Hedgeman, a Minnesotan who had helped to organize the March on Washington along with A. Philip Randolph and Bayard Rustin. Her approach balanced extreme protest methods with more moderate approaches that could be then embraced to bring success.

Around the time of Dr. King's assassination, Black students had been demanding better conditions at colleges and universities around the country, including at the University of Minnesota. U of M students reported that in addition to African American history being left out of the curriculum, they endured constant insults and other indignities that left them feeling like outcasts rather than legitimate students seeking education. They couldn't live in dormitories, campus social life was closed to them, and there wasn't anything in the curriculum that reflected their experience or our history. Dr. John Wright, a proud young scholar I knew well and a fourth-generation Minnesotan, was a student at the time. He became so frustrated that talented Black students elected to attend historically Black colleges and universities in the South rather than the University of Minnesota that in the mid-1960s he decided to take it upon himself to recruit students door to door in Minneapolis's black neighborhoods. However, the university wasn't offering any incentives for Blacks to enroll or pursue a degree, causing John to join with other students to form the Afro-American Action Committee in 1967.

The group drafted a list of demands and met with University President Malcolm Moos and other officials, but it didn't take long for the students to feel that the talks weren't going to go anywhere. They issued a twenty-four-hour deadline, and when the deadline passed with no response from university administration, on January 14, 1969, seven of the students walked into the student records office in Morrill Hall, the university's administration building, and refused to leave.

That action caught the attention of both university officials and the community. I joined in with my dear friend Mahmoud El-Kati who had been a resource for the students and community to support those students' efforts. Thankfully, President Moos took the students' demands for African American courses seriously and made a conscious decision to create an environment of acceptance and support among university administrators, department chairs, faculty, and the Board of Regents. From this effort, a committee of African American educators developed the African American Studies Program in record time, and by the fall of 1969, course offerings were available to students. Vice President Paul Cashman and Assistant Vice President Fred E. Lukermann were particularly helpful in making this happen.

The history and struggle of major academic institutions accepting African American studies as both a curriculum and a department in the late 1960s and early 1970s met with mixed results. After Dr. King's assassination there were protests by students on many campuses, including some historically Black colleges and universities, that included efforts toward the creation of such academic programs. For instance, students at Howard University held a sit-in and rally to protest the Vietnam War and ROTC recruitment, in addition to demanding an African American studies program. At the same time, members of the Afro-American Student Union at the University of California, Berkeley, proposed the creation of a four-year interdisciplinary degree program. Students at Berkeley submitted their proposal to the school's chancellor, who then created a new administrative post and appointed the well-known Black sociologist Dr. Andrew Billingsley to assist the students in developing their plan. Their first courses were offered in 1970. I was also successful in getting the University of Minnesota to award academic credits to the inmates at Stillwater Prison for taking the courses we taught through The Way.

Like UC Berkeley, the University of Minnesota didn't put up any barriers, and we were able to create a strong program that was accessible to our students. I was appointed to teach two courses, *Black Families in White America* and *African Americans in the Welfare System*. Having met Dr. Billingsley at an Urban League conference in 1968, and being very impressed with his work leading to his groundbreaking book *Black Families in White America*, I invited him to Minneapolis to help me develop the department's Black Families curriculum. He graciously agreed.

It is important to note that we have a long history of courses taught in many colleges and universities on the history, culture, and politics of our people. Scholars such as W. E. B. Du Bois, Charles S. Johnson, John Hope Franklin, E. Franklin Frazier, Carter G. Woodson, Herbert Aptheker, C. L. R. James, Vincent Harding, Nathan Hare, Geneva Smitherman, and Melissa Harris-Perry were among those who created and refined systematic ways of studying and teaching African American contributions and experiences in America, such as the Black Arts Movement, Black Power movements, the identification of our heritage, as well as other ways of understanding and appreciating African culture and the experience of Africans in America. But the work of those scholars was not being taught widely in the 1960s and 1970s. Black students at the University of Minnesota demanded a role in both studying and offering that rich scholarship in the form of an academic discipline available to all students.

The African American Studies Department planners were very cognizant of the battle for Black and urban history to be taught both in the academy and in schools. Aware of the shifting back and forth of efforts to integrate, and to teach Black children their history as well as to have it included in higher education curricula, the idea of *town versus gown* became an important concept and objective as discussions among students, community activists, administrators, and academics developed around curriculum, scholarship, and the philosophy of the African American Studies Department at the University of Minnesota. Belief in the value of "bringing the town"—incorporating community experiences into the academy—had a strong following while the department was being organized. Scholars, activists, researchers, graduate students, and individuals from the broader community were encouraged to submit applications to teach in the department. Many of us engaged in the process had high hopes that this approach would produce scholars who would be knowledgeable about African American people. There needed to be acknowledgment by universities that African American studies was legitimate and parallel to any other department of study these institutions already supported.

We began a search for a department chair, and I was able to persuade Lillian Anthony, director of the Minneapolis Civil Rights Department, to serve as acting chair until we could hire a permanent person. In the meantime, we drafted the founding documents for the department. Mahmoud El-Kati was one of the founding participants in this development and believed strongly that the basis for the department should be driven by morality rather than politics; it was important, he felt, to search for a leader who was idealistic and self-less—a scholar who was committed to the education of our students rather than someone who was motivated by money or politics.

Our search did not yield a large pool of candidates, but Lillian Anthony recommended Dr. George King who was a friend of hers. He was selected to become chair in 1970.

After the creation of the African American Studies Department in 1971, I was elected to the University of Minnesota's Board of Regents, becoming the first Black person to hold this position. I was a candidate for one of the three at-large positions that were available at the time. I would learn from a newspaper announcement, however, that a lot of politicking took place in the committees during the selection process. Representative Martin Olav Sabo managed the process that led to my being elected.

Looking back, I am sure that my long-standing work with the DFL leadership along with my participation in political activities, discussions, and strategies made me a desirable candidate to become the first Black regent. I had worked with Senator Donald Fraser during the passage of Fair Housing legislation, and I knew Representative Sabo who ran for Fraser's seat in the House of Representatives when he stepped down to run for his state senate position. Representative Robert (Bob) Latz and Senator John (Jack) Davies were also among the state senators that I knew.

I also knew State Senator and Lieutenant Governor Sandy Keith, who served under Governor Karl Rolvaag. Sandy decided to run against Governor Rolvaag as the DFL candidate for governor in 1966 and asked me to be on his team in some capacity. He suggested state auditor. Chuck and I shared a good laugh at that suggestion because, as Chuck pointed out, I had a hard enough time managing our family finances. Besides, we both agreed that our children were too young for me to consider the level of involvement it would take to serve on a governor's cabinet.

I was honored to have been invited to sit on this august board, but it soon became apparent that there would be problems with the new chair of the African American Studies Department, with regard to my appointment. I had been a faculty member of the African American Studies Department since its inception and had resigned upon my election to the Board of Regents. During my first few months as a regent, I observed cronyism and other problems in the department. The chair was not hiring enough high-quality teachers to staff the department within the time frame required by the university and was not fulfilling the demands of the student protestors. We had worked so hard—and the students had sacrificed so much to get the department approved—that I felt an obligation to visit with the chair and express my concerns.

Following what I thought was a clarifying and honest conversation, the department chair wrote a letter to President Moos accusing me of interfering with the department and not resigning from the department correctly, suggesting that such action was causing budget problems. President Moos shared the chair's letter with me and offered a resolution to the charges—for me to write my resignation letter from the department. I did, and it was dated and worded to dispute the chair's allegations.

To the relief of those of us who designed the African American Studies Department, George King left the university in 1974 and was replaced by Dr. Geneva Southall, who had joined the department in 1970 as a professor of Black music studies. Also, as a music scholar she taught graduate courses in the Department of Music and wrote three books on Thomas "Blind Tom" Wiggins, the famed slave pianist and composer of the 1800s.

Two other scholars I want to recognize are Earl Craig, who taught political science in the department from 1970–72 and at the School of Public Affairs from 1972–1973; and, of course, I was thrilled when Dr. John S. Wright, who was one of the major forces in the student movement, began teaching in the department. He would later become chair of the department and a nationally recognized scholar among whose many accomplishments is principal scholar of the prestigious Archie Givens Sr. Collection of African American Literature that is housed at the University of Minnesota. The collection contains more than ten thousand books, magazines, and pamphlets by or about African Americans.

Because we were both new to the board, Regent Loanne Thrane and I became a traveling team, visiting the university's campuses throughout the state to listen to students, faculty, and staff. I was particularly sensitive to the minority composition and population on each campus we visited. I was also very interested in knowing about all departments and special programs under the responsibility of the president and the Board of Regents, and I chose to serve on several committees during my tenure on the board: the Faculty, Staff, and Student Affairs Committee; the Health Sciences Committee; and the Budget and Executive committees.

The Faculty, Staff, and Student Affairs Committee oversaw personnel and programs involving faculty, staff, and students at the university. I thought that service on that committee would help me understand the university's system relating to those units. I also chaired the Student Concerns Committee.

The Health Sciences Committee had supervision over the policies, programs, and planning in the health sciences. I was chair of that committee with the assistance of Paul H. Cashman, Vice President for Student Affairs, one of the men who had been so helpful in getting the African American Studies Department up and running. My service on that committee was during the early stages of the development of magnetic imaging (MRI) technology. My discussions centered on the wisdom of having that very expensive equipment in all hospitals, including the U of M hospital. I remember suggesting that the equipment could be shared with regional hospitals, saving money and sharing resources.

When I became a regent, the Morris campus was experimenting with an excellent recruitment program for Black students under the direction of Dr. William B. Steward, an MIT-trained electrical engineer. The program he led was patterned after a program established in Chicago that was very successful in recruiting, retaining, and graduating minority students. I continued to support his work and participated in many events on the Morris campus and was commencement speaker during one of the years that I was a regent.

Being the only African American on the Board of Regents was interesting. I learned quickly that my suggestions and observations were not immediately heard or acknowledged. However, if a white male member repeated what I had said, the words were heard. I have heard many other Blacks and women express that same sentiment in their professional experiences. Not only that, but the board was surprised that my interests were broader than only minority issues and concerns. I wanted to know about fish and wildlife, and I was interested in agriculture and all other fields of study, but the members seemed to only ask and listen when I talked about diversity issues. This was very disappointing—so much so that I began to question my communication skills. Later, when I went to the University of Massachusetts to complete my graduate studies, I took a course in communications skills and learned from my classmates that my skills were well developed. It wasn't that I wasn't communicating well with my colleagues on the Board of Regents: rather, I believe it was their inability or refusal to listen to an African American whose thinking was broader than what they were willing to accept.

However, that didn't stop the progressive work I wanted

to do. One of many things I remain very proud of is that during my tenure on the board we encouraged student engagement in regents' meetings. Eventually, students were elected
as student regents. In addition, meetings became more open
to the public, and space for public observance of board meetings was enlarged.

My service on the Board of Regents ended in 1974 when
Chuck was transferred to Denver. The board was disappointed that I was leaving, but before I left, the chair, Governor Elmer Andersen, and the board kindly honored me with
regent emeritus status. My title became Emeritus/Emeriti
Regent Josie R. Johnson, and I was given the full benefits of
a completed six-year term. I was also encouraged to put forth
names of individuals who might replace me. I submitted a
few names, and the governor selected Wenda Moore.

10

COLORADO
AND NEW CHALLENGES

WHEN CHUCK WAS ASSIGNED to manage Honeywell's operations in Denver, he had already worked at Honeywell for nearly eighteen years, and his advancement had been slow by comparison with his white peers. Chuck's management and problem-solving abilities were well known and respected within the company, and he now had responsibilities that involved training managers. I had served on the Board of Regents for three years and had resolved to resign my position to move to Colorado. I was honored with the same benefits that all full-term regents received. A few of my white feminist friends questioned my decision, as it was inconsistent with their view of women's progress. In contrast, I always viewed the Black struggle as a people's struggle—not the struggle of a single gender—and even though my election to the Board had been historic, it never occurred to me that the position had more value than my family.

In November 1974, our family prepared to move to Denver. Patrice was in her sophomore year at Fisk, so the move would not affect her. Josie was completing ninth grade and at the end of her junior high experience. Norrene, however, was in her senior year of high school; I did not want the move to interfere with her graduation, so I contacted the superintendents of the two school districts involved, and we were able to make arrangements between school systems to ensure that Norrene would earn the credits she needed in Denver to graduate on time and be able to return to Minnesota to march with her classmates at Bloomington Jefferson High School.

We sold the house in Bloomington and in Denver bought a beautiful home on a quiet street in the Hampden South neighborhood, southeast of downtown. It was an ethnically mixed neighborhood near several integrated housing developments and townhouses. Our house had three bedrooms, four bathrooms, three fireplaces including one in the master bedroom, a two-car garage, and a swimming pool. Somehow I came to be in charge of looking after the swimming pool even though I was not the family swimmer. I had not been fond of swimming since my childhood when I once had a scare with drowning while out crabbing with my mother in Texas. But Chuck swam and the girls had taken lessons in Minnesota and were excellent swimmers.

One of our neighbors and a schoolmate of the girls, Michael Winslow, distinguished himself in our new neighborhood with his ability to make all manner of sounds with his voice. He would sit out in his family's open garage across the street from our house and practice making sounds loud enough to be heard throughout the whole neighborhood: sirens, cards, guns, you name it. His abilities earned him a career. Later, we learned that Michael had made a successful television and movie career using his talents on *The Gong Show* and in movies like *Spaceballs* and the *Police Academy* films.

Soon after we got settled in Denver, Chuck and the girls got into their routines of work and school, and I went about the business of taking care of the house, preparing meals, and walking our German shepherd, Enye, around the neighborhood. For the first time in my adult life, I didn't have meetings and other obligations, and I found myself free to indulge in interests like my love of skiing. Chuck and I had taken some free ski lessons at Hyland Lake Park while we still lived in Minnesota, and we had also taken a ski trip to Aspen years earlier. We had learned about the national Black Ski Club and the many Black skiers who gathered each year in Colorado. It was on that Aspen trip that we had once mistakenly caught the wrong chairlift, one that went to the top of a high mountain. As the lift continued its climb, we recognized that the slope we were heading for was much too advanced for us. I was so scared when we got off at the top. The sky was getting dark and the snow was blowing all around us. I didn't know how we were going to get down, and I just knew that we were going to die up there. After a few moments Chuck, being the engineer, determined that we would just take it slowly and cut a wide path back and forth down the steep slope, stopping as we needed. Our descent took a couple of hours, but to my relief we made it down the mountain safely.

I also learned that a family I had known well in Houston now lived in Denver, and we reconnected. These friends regularly invited me to go with them to the parks; the husband was on the ski patrol, and it was his job to go around to the public parks and check on the conditions of the ski routes. The three of us would head out in the mornings to places like Winter Park, to the west of Denver. He would go off to work, and his wife and I would take our skis and play. Having grown up with relatively consistent weather in Houston, I loved the change in seasons, and the sunlight in Colorado had a magical quality, especially during the winter months. The opportunity to ski—and often—felt like a dream come true.

Otherwise, it seems that my being at home as much as I was in those early days in Denver proved to be more of an adjustment for the family than the overall move from Minnesota itself. Eventually, Norrene and Josie sat me down and said, "Mother, *please* get busy. You are driving us crazy. You pick up and wash our clothes, keep our rooms clean, serve meals on time. And you want to spend time talking when we get home!" This was not at all what they were used to, and they were serious in their encouragement that I get out of the house and engage with my new community.

Soon after this conversation with the girls, I met Arie Taylor. Arie had become the first African American woman to be elected to the Colorado State House of Representatives in 1972 and would eventually go on to serve six terms. Arie had lived in Denver since 1958, was very knowledgeable, had deep relationships, and had developed a reputation as a fierce advocate for the community. She had a forceful and direct style and was clearly committed to improving the lives of Black people and women. I liked her immediately and began to go with her to meetings in the community.

One day, Arie and I went to a nursery school in Denver and she told me about the Era of Reducing Child Poverty, day-care legislation that had been introduced in the Colorado Senate by State Senator George L. Brown. This legislation was part of a national movement to enhance the quality of education and expand the rights of minorities, people with disabilities, children, and youth. George and Arie needed help lobbying for the bill in the Colorado legislature, and I discovered that my experience lobbying in Minnesota was suddenly relevant here in my new home. I volunteered and found myself once again in the halls of a state capitol working to improve the lives of people and community.

Arie introduced me to Senator Brown, a handsome, soft-spoken Black man who exuded a niceness that reminded me of Minnesotans. A Democrat who had been in the legislature for nineteen years, Senator Brown had trained as a journalist and directed the Denver Housing Authority prior to taking office. Our views aligned on many issues. In 1975, in the middle of his fifth senate term, Senator Brown decided to run for lieutenant governor. I volunteered with his team and offered additional campaign strategies that had been effective in Minnesota. Eventually, George asked me to become his campaign manager.

As a newcomer to the state, volunteering to work on the campaign, I felt very welcome and encouraged. This encouragement and support came from people who had worked with Senator Brown all his political life. Our campaign was successful, and George became the first Black person elected lieutenant governor in the United States since Reconstruction. (Incidentally, five African American lieutenant governors were elected during the years of Reconstruction, 1863–1877.) Within an hour, Mervyn M. Dymally added to this accomplishment by becoming the first Black lieutenant governor in the State of California.

In organizing his office as lieutenant governor, George appointed me to be his chief of staff. He continued his campaign's focus on diversity, equity, and justice, and this fit perfectly with my administrative experience and history. My job was to do everything that I could to support the implementation of George's agenda as lieutenant governor, which included promoting the community's awareness of and connection with his work.

I am pleased to say that the staff in our office was very diverse. Unfortunately, this diversity was not reflected in the physical halls of the capitol, in the state's vendor contracts, or in Colorado lawmakers' understanding of the diverse communities living within the state. During my tenure, I helped to convene the Minority Art Committee to introduce artistic representations of Colorado's Native, African American, Asian, and Latino communities at the state capitol. To chair this committee, I recruited Robert Ragland, a Black Coloradan visual artist whom I had met through my work organizing a Delta annual convention in Denver. I have always appreciated Bob Ragland's work and to this day have several of his paintings on the walls of my condominium. During George's tenure, the committee succeeded in commissioning a bust by the accomplished sculptor Ed Dwight of the lieutenant governor, in mounting several exhibits, and in hanging works by minority artists in the state capitol.

Soon after we set up office, we learned of the challenges that minority businesses had in getting contracts with the State of Colorado for services like road construction, repair of state buildings, and bridge building. There had been little transparency up until then in sharing the basic processes for applying for contracts with the state, and there were no examples of minority businesses receiving contracts. In response, our office organized a conference to assist minority firms in negotiating the system for securing contracts. This two-day conference brought in representatives from around Colorado to discuss the type of work that was needed as well as the specifics around the bidding and application processes for these contracts. As a result of this conference and other actions taken by our office, many minority contractors were better able to compete and succeed in doing business with the state.

Marilyn Youngbird, a young Native American woman and tribal member of the Arikara and Hidatsa Nations, came to work in the office of the lieutenant governor. Marilyn carried the wisdom of her culture behind her quiet confidence and contagious smile. At the time, state legislators knew very little about the plight of American Indians in Colorado and in fact were in the process of being defrauded by a white imposter who called himself Billy Jack. He dressed complete with a belt, knife, and other Native symbols, and he spoke with an accent as he convinced legislators to allocate financial support to an Indian survival program that he would manage. Marilyn spoke to the legislature and was instrumental in exposing Billy Jack as a fraud. We were alarmed when he subsequently came to our office threatening to kill Marilyn. We notified security and spent many days behind locked entry doors. After this incident, the governor and lieutenant governor created a new Commission on Indian Affairs and recommended Marilyn to head it. In her work as commissioner, Marilyn was able to bring the suffering of Native tribes in Colorado before lawmakers and to advocate for the allocation of funds in support of restoring and strengthening the Ute Mountain and Southern Ute tribes.

In those days, capitol security had advised public officials and their staff to be on the lookout for anything that seemed suspicious around the building. Early one morning, I arrived to open the office and found a strange package on the receptionist's desk. The package looked official with a postal label but the return address on the box was unclear. When the receptionist and other staff members began to arrive, they looked the package over, but no one knew how the box had arrived at the office or anything about it. I decided to call security and in short order a security guard came to the office. We stood at a distance as he peeled back the brown paper top of the box. There was a quiet release of pressure from within the box, and nails, shredded paper, and pieces of glass sprang through the opening and spread over the surface of the desk. The box had clearly been rigged to hurt the person who opened it, but thankfully the security guard was not harmed. The guard gathered up the box and its malevolent contents and took it out of the office. The members of our staff looked at each other in disbelief and began talking, consoling one another. All through the incident, I had been worried about the staff and felt the weight of my responsibility for their safety. What if someone had been hurt? I was so thankful that we had received warnings from security. I felt a deep sense of relief that we had followed protocol and that no one had been injured.

• • •

Early in his campaign, I received a call at our office notifying us that presidential candidate Jimmy Carter was planning to visit Denver. At this point in his campaign, Carter arrived with just one staff person and no fanfare. We knew very little about Carter then, just that he was a peanut farmer, the governor of Georgia, and was considered a long shot to win. Both the lieutenant governor and I were scheduled for other commitments during the time of his visit, so I asked State Representative Wellington Webb if he would be willing to meet with the candidate and help familiarize him with the political landscape in the state. Wellington was a native of Denver and very politically astute. I believe that the two of them hit it off, because Wellington went on to head Carter's campaign in Colorado. After winning the election, Carter asked Wellington to serve as his regional director for the U.S. Department of Health and Human Services.

Looking back, I must say that the racism and controversies that I experienced while serving with Lieutenant Governor Brown exposed me to how white supremacy could be expressed in politics. As the first Black person to hold statewide office in Colorado, George did not have an easy time. From the beginning, Governor Richard Lamm seemed reluctant to have George on the ticket—even though George had won his seat in the statewide primary election. In Colorado, the governor is elected in a separate campaign from the lieutenant governor. Entering his position, George had a chilly reception from Lamm, and they did not get along. In addition, George was under constant scrutiny while in his position and was twice accused of mismanaging funds for his office. As a member of his staff, in another one of the most frightening experiences of my life, I was deposed as part of a grand jury investigation. In this case, the accounting discrepancies in question were determined to be clerical errors related to his travel expenses, and no charges were filed. Later, in 1978, the governor accused George of overspending his department budget by $10,000 and withheld his pay-check. Brown sued the governor and the case was ultimately settled—but as his chief of staff, I learned to pay very close attention to the details of our budgets and expenditures. In spite of the conflicts with Governor Lamm and the petty and serious ways in which racism was manifest in our experiences while in office, we were able to accomplish many of our goals, especially in creating a welcoming and responsive environment for diverse communities. Unfortunately, the experience greatly frustrated George Brown. He served only one four-year term as lieutenant governor and did not seek public office again.

I met many passionately engaged people during my time working at the Colorado State Capitol and living in Denver, people who not only generously shared their knowledge and experience of the state with me but also inspired my hope and expanded my commitment to the struggle of Black people. We shared a belief in the strength of our African American heritage and the possibility of justice, and we were all working in various ways to uplift, educate, and politically engage our community.

One of my dearest friends in Denver was a woman named Rachel Noel. She was a Fiskite, a Delta, and the first African American to serve on the Denver Public Schools Board of Education. In 1968, Rachel had presented a resolution to the school board to develop a plan for the integration of the Denver city school district. It took two years for the Noel Resolution to pass, and during that time Rachel and her family regularly received threatening phone calls and mail. While I lived in Denver, Rachel was elected to the University of Colorado Board of Regents; she and I taught together at Metropolitan State College of Denver. We co-taught Black history and the course on Black families in white America that I had developed at the University of Minnesota. I have fond memories of sitting in front of the bay window at Rachel's home planning our curriculum, discussing Black history and culture, and conferring about the development and introduction of African American curricula at academic institutions. She was an important confidant for me and we discussed the racism and many other experiences I had while serving in George Brown's office.

I had other friendships that were important sustenance for me during my years in Colorado. After I had completed my service in the lieutenant governor's office, a good friend of George Brown's named Ann Nickerson and I began spending more time together. Although Ann was not political, she was a social worker, and her work with and commitment to children and families in Colorado gifted her with deep insights that she generously shared with me.

Larry Borum was someone I had known in Minnesota when he served at the St. Paul Urban League, and we reconnected after he moved to Colorado to take up the position of president and CEO of the Urban League of Metropolitan Denver. Our time together in Denver always felt like a joyous family reunion, a transplanted piece of Minnesota. Larry went on to head Denver's Agency for Human Rights and Community Relations, and he persisted as a strong community advocate for Black teachers and students in Colorado.

I also met Gloria Travis Tanner through a family relative shortly after we moved to Denver. Gloria would eventually become the first African American woman elected to the Colorado state senate. Gloria was a Delta who became a trusted adviser for me, and an important sounding board in helping me understand the politics and culture in Colorado.

In the 1970s, Black women were busy establishing African American political and cultural institutions in Denver, and there were two organizations in particular that impressed and engaged me. In 1977, Colorado Black Women for Political Action organized to meaningfully engage Black people and

Black women in particular in political processes. I was honored when they invited me to speak at their first luncheon. This organization involved many of the people with whom I had worked closely while in the lieutenant governor's office, people like Regis Groff, who would become the second Black state senator in Colorado. Regis was a respected educator, very rational, and we always relied on him to provide us with alternative perspectives on issues being discussed.

In Denver's art scene at that time, I was so moved by the work of dancer Cleo Parker Robinson. When I lived in the city, her dance studio was still fledgling, but the quality and impact of her artistry and her commitment to uplifting the African American community through dance made a lasting impact on me. Her nonprofit dance company has continued in its stated mission to teach "generations of families the beauty, fun, and healing power of dance" for nearly fifty years.

Anna Jo Haynes and her daughter Allegra "Happy" Haynes were also active in Colorado Black Women for Political Action. Anna Jo had been an old friend and adviser to George Brown, and Happy Haynes had become a staff assistant in our office soon after her graduation from college. The lieutenant governor was interested in establishing an open-door policy to encourage community members to bring their concerns to our office. To advance this initiative, we created the position of ombudsman, and Happy was promoted to this new role. Happy went on to become a member of the Colorado State Legislature, to serve as deputy mayor of Denver in 2017, and she continues to provide important counsel to Denver's mayors and public officials to this day.

In Colorado, I found my leadership opportunities continuing to expand, both with organizations that I had long known like Delta Sigma Theta, and with new organizations like National Public Radio. The Deltas put my organizational skills to good use when I became the coordinator for the 34th

Delta Sigma Theta National Convention in August 1977. This event was held in Denver and featured Natalie Cole as entertainment. It was an important demonstration of the creativity, intelligence, and strength of the Black community in Colorado. That same year, I was invited to become the first Black woman to join the board of National Public Radio. I had been an early subscriber to public radio in Minnesota and was pleased to have the opportunity to serve on this national board under the leadership of Frank Mankiewicz, alongside Alex Haley, Bill Moyers, and others.

While my engagements in my Colorado community developed and deepened, at home Chuck and I were becoming more distant from one another. In our first year in Colorado, Norrene graduated and headed off to Spelman College. Josie graduated from high school in 1976 and left for college at Harvard. Chuck and I had always thought that when the girls left home, we would have more time together, but instead we both ended up filling the space created by the girls' departures with more work and other commitments. Chuck was always supportive of my crazy lifestyle and a dedicated father to the girls. As we noticed that we weren't choosing to spend more time with each other, Chuck and I had many private conversations, trying to think through what was happening in our marriage. In reflecting on our life together, Chuck wondered what more one could want: we had been very successful at raising our children, establishing a comfortable home and life, and were even good friends to one another. Still, I recognized that I did not feel cherished or loved romantically in our marriage. And even though Chuck may not have been fully satisfied in our relationship, he could not rationalize ending it. Ultimately, I could no longer deny the dissatisfactions that I felt—I believed there had to be something more and registered the need to make a change.

This was a very difficult time for me. I was not of a

generation that sought outside counsel for private matters, and I had not grown up in an environment where I could talk about these things with other people. I had no idea that other people faced similar challenges in their relationships and that what Chuck and I experienced was actually not unusual. At that time, I was also not aware of the concept of stages of growth in personal development or in relationships. Years later, I read the work of cultural anthropologist Margaret Mead and found tremendous resonance with her ideas of how human beings move through developmental stages, growing and changing over their lifespan as part of a natural process. This insight was really helpful for me in making some sense of what had happened in my relationship with Chuck.

After a trial separation, Chuck and I would finalize our divorce in 1982. Chuck was always very fair and took care of all the details. I worried most that I was disappointing my children. Whether the girls were vocal about it or not at the time, I do not believe that they truly understood my choice. Similarly, some aspects of what happened in my marriage remain a mystery even to me. Who can say what would have happened if I had held on to the relationship? At the time, I felt certain that staying was not an option. As it was, I chose to leave and go where my spirit and instincts took me. It is true that my choice for growth involved pain and loss, but it also ushered me into new possibilities and a deeper experience of my own self. For this, I am thankful.

11

BACK TO SCHOOL

I WAS READY TO LEAVE COLORADO and was contemplating where to go when a delegation of recruiters from Fisk University came to Denver. As Chuck and I were working through our decision to go separate ways, we hosted a reception for the Fisk recruits at our home and invited our friends and colleagues from the community, many of whom were also Fiskites. The recruiters' visit reminded me of a long-standing dream I had—to formalize the national network of Fisk Clubs into an alumni association. I had been a very active alumna and remained in contact with many Fisk graduates through my work and travels.

Fisk had always felt like home to me. Chuck and I had met there. My brothers, my daughter Patrice, and my nephew had all gone to Fisk. With the changes in my professional and personal life in Colorado, I found that I now had time to focus on this dream. I packed up a few personal belongings and resolved to return to Fisk to be of service. One of the visiting recruiters, Dr. George Neely, a tenured professor of physics at the university, generously offered to host me at his home in Tennessee while I was getting settled.

Many changes had taken place in and around Fisk in the twenty-eight years since I had graduated. Most notably, I was struck by the differences in the students. These students were not the World War II veterans who grew up under Jim Crow with whom I had gone to school. After the decision in *Brown v. the Board of Education* and after the protests and marches for civil rights of the 1960s and 1970s, many at Fisk were first-generation college students. They were freer in their personal expression and lifestyles—and they brought different sets of experiences and sensibilities to the school. Suffice it to say, they were not wearing the white gloves and formal dress that my classmates and I had counted as basic decorum.

Fisk, like many of the historically Black colleges and universities, was struggling to maintain its student population. Many white Ivy League universities had begun to recruit Black students and offer scholarships, advantages, and opportunities that Black colleges and universities could not offer, and Black students were choosing to attend mainstream and elite majority-white schools. This shift exacerbated the financial challenges faced by many schools like Fisk. Black colleges and universities had long served as oases for the development of Black minds and for the preservation of Black history and culture even when mainstream white educational institutions were not open to Black students. Fisk's public financial struggles at the time of my return to campus made the need to raise money from alumni, supporting the school and creating student scholarships, that much more important.

Eager for my new assignment, I embarked upon researching the legal steps necessary for the university to create an association. A formal alumni association could organize the Fisk Clubs to work together, to raise funds, and to align their member networks in strong support of the school. Fisk University staff and the Chicago Fisk Club members were of great assistance to me, as I had never written a constitution and bylaws for an association.

In 1980, we were successful in obtaining the approval of the University Board of Trustees, and I became the first president of the Fisk University Alumni Association, a position I served in for two years. Harold Kelly, Class of 1958 and the president of the Chicago Club, then became the next president. Harold had been part of Fisk's early-entry program, coming to the university around age fifteen, as he had been able to take university-level classes while still in high school. Harold was very efficient and hard-working and held the group together for more than fifteen years. We strongly believed that the alumni association would become important for recruiting new students for Fisk—organizing alumni clubs on a regional basis, holding social and business gatherings during annual commencement activities at the university, and preparing alumni to serve as ambassadors, among many other ways.

Around this same time, my brother Judson decided to run for the Texas 18th District congressional seat that had been left by Barbara Jordan when she stepped down due to illness. Barbara Jordan had been the first African American elected to the Texas Senate after Reconstruction and then went on to represent Texas in the U.S. Congress. Our families had long been friends, and Barbara had always been very serious, very smart, and very clear about the issues. Judson felt close to Barbara and followed her career. Mickey Leland and Anthony Hall were also mounting campaigns to compete for Barbara Jordan's seat. Judson had just been reelected to the Houston City Council, and several family members and I had been active in his campaign. When Judson declared his candidacy for Barbara's position, I continued to offer support as office manager and supervisor for the new campaign. Unfortunately, the voters who had just elected Judson to the city council did not support his congressional run, and Mickey Leland was elected to take the open seat and went on to serve for several terms. My daughter Patrice would eventually serve as Mickey Leland's chief of staff.

While I was at Fisk, I was also given the opportunity to

be of service to my sorority, Delta Sigma Theta. I had been initiated into the Alpha Beta Chapter in 1950. In the years following my graduation, I had always found great resonance between the values with which I'd grown up and the values that were at the heart of the Delta sisterhood. I remained active in the sorority and in my relationships with fellow Delta sisters throughout the country. After my return to Nashville in 1979, the Delta's National Membership and Intake Committee asked me to serve as an adviser to the Alpha Beta Chapter at Fisk. By this point, the sorority had been incorporated for sixty-seven years, and I had been a Delta for nearly thirty years.

During this period, initiation practices at fraternities and sororities were growing increasingly extreme, and stories of hazing deaths on college campuses in North Carolina, Pennsylvania, and Louisiana had been in the news. I recall how anxious my brother and I were even as my nephew rushed the Omega Psi Phi fraternity. I also thought that some of the hazing that was happening at Black fraternities and sororities was symptomatic of an oppressed people consciously or unconsciously acting out by taking on the characteristics of their oppressors.

That year, there was a group of young women interested in joining the Alpha Beta Chapter. The women complained of initiation activities that were at odds with the sorority's values of service and sisterhood. I was on campus and available to be of assistance when the national headquarters determined that the chapter intake committee at Fisk would benefit from some clarity and reinforcement of the mission and principles of Delta Sigma Theta. When I learned of some of the activities, I had a deep concern that Black women in general and my sorority sisters in particular were forgetting who they were and from whence they came.

I began to attend the intake committee meetings for the Alpha Beta Chapter as elder and adviser. I think that my best service was to remind them of Delta's value of sisterhood and what it meant. As a public service sorority, Delta Sigma Theta was founded to promote academic excellence and provide assistance to those in need. The organization was built on the shoulders of women of character and caliber, women like the twenty-two founders whose first public act was to participate in the Women's Suffrage March in Washington, D.C., in 1913. I reminded the intake committee members that as Deltas they shared in the legacy of Dorothy Height and many others and that they themselves had an important role to play in continuing the leadership and service contributions of the sisterhood to the Black community.

I am pleased to say that at least for that group of young women, the Alpha Beta Chapter initiation practices were reformed. The young women successfully pledged Delta and developed a close feeling of sisterhood. To this day, I am blessed to be in touch with several of those Fisk sorority sisters and to be honored with a special elder role. I was elected to the National Board of Delta Sigma Theta and served on the executive committee; I was also chair of Arts and Letters from 1983 to 1988. In 1985, we had a very successful Arts and Letters Renaissance in Dallas that featured poet Nikki Giovanni, singer Bill Withers, and the artwork of Clementine Hunter and Earl Hooks, among others. Delta Sigma Theta continues to be the largest African American Greek-lettered organization, and I am still today a dues-paying member and a sorority elder, classified as a Delta Dear.

I was still in Tennessee during the end of the Jimmy Carter/ Walter Mondale presidential election campaign against Ronald Reagan in 1979. The campaign came through Nashville, and I made arrangements to visit with Carter and Mondale. At this point, Walter had been my friend for nearly twenty years in the civil rights struggle, and we were very aligned in our values and worldviews. I offered to become involved in the campaign and to do outreach in the Black communities of Tennessee and Kentucky. My daughter Patrice had been a student intern assigned to Tennessee Representative Alvin King when she was a student at Fisk, and I knew several Tennessee state legislators. I felt comfortable with my understanding of the political infrastructure in Tennessee and with the prospect of working in the Black communities in the two states. The campaign work was hard and long and ultimately unsuccessful, as Black voters in Tennessee and Kentucky did not turn out in support of Carter and Mondale. For long afterward, I felt a deep sense of guilt and responsibility that my work had not brought the outcome for which I had hoped.

Many years later, in 2015, during a yearlong series of events honoring the life and legacy of Vice President Mondale, I was invited to the Four Seasons Hotel in Washington, D.C., to participate in a panel discussion about the civil rights struggle. That evening included a reception, dinner, and a discussion between Vice President Mondale and President Jimmy Carter. At this event, I sat at a table assigned to the participants in the daylong activities. I was surprised and thrilled to have the opportunity to visit person-to-person with President Carter. I reminded him that I had campaigned on his behalf in Tennessee and Kentucky. I will always remember that evening and our conversation.

In 1981, I applied to pursue my doctoral studies in education administration at the University of Massachusetts at Amherst. Based on observations that I'd made while consulting in the public schools in Minneapolis, I was interested in researching how to create an environment that would help African American students be successful in their K–12 experiences and beyond. I applied with the encouragement of my colleague Lillian Anthony and the support of Norma Jean Andersen, who was the dean of the college of education at

Amherst, whom I had first met in the early 1960s when she served as an evaluator for a federal training program for parents, paraprofessionals, and teachers in Twin Cities schools.

Norma Jean offered me a lovely room in her home until student housing became available. Her family was very active and engaged in the Amherst community: her husband was a church minister and community activist, and her four children were artists, writers, educators, musicians, and Christian ministers. Norma Jean's home was a welcoming place, and I settled in. I shared many meals and lively conversations with Norma Jean, her husband, and children, and I felt as though I really was one of the family.

The chance to return to school at the age of fifty-one I recognized as a rich and exciting time in my life. I was delighted to find myself on campus with students from all over the world, particularly those from the continent of Africa. Even though I was the oldest student in various groups, I appreciated the experiences and maturity of many of the other students studying education administration. We would gather regularly to share what we were learning and to advise each other in our work. Some students were researching the emotional development of African American students while others focused more closely in my area of study, the role of parents and community in supporting and advancing the education of Black children. One of my closest friends and classmates was Ruby Burges, a respected curriculum development consultant in her nonstudent life. These relationships would become close and lasting friendships.

I was eager to get deep into the research on the education of African American children and to talk with scholars who shared my interests. At Amherst, I met professors who had been in the field of education for a long time and with whom I would spend many hours talking about what should be included in a curriculum for African American students. Meyer Weinberg, a scholar of W. E. B. Du Bois, was the chair of my dissertation committee. He was a distinguished scholar and one of the pioneer researchers of integrated education following the Civil Rights Act of 1964. His eighteen books included *The World of W.E.B. Du Bois,* a journey through Du Bois's views on virtually all aspects of twentieth-century life and other studies of the education of poor and minority children. W.E.B. was my hero. Both Du Bois and Meyer emphasized the particular necessity for African American people to understand their history and context. Benefiting from Meyer's scholarship and historical work was a dream come true for me.

The papers of W.E.B. Du Bois were held in the special collections and university archives at Amherst, the library that in 1994 would take on his name. I will never forget the first time I stood outside that twenty-eight-story building. In some ways, that experience mirrored the first time I saw Jubilee Hall as an entering freshman at Fisk. To me, both of those buildings represented the phenomenal history of our people: Jubilee Hall was the reminder of a people who believed in education, who sacrificed and shared their talents to make education available to so many African American people; the W.E.B. Du Bois library represented a scholar who gained knowledge and pride of Black people while at Fisk and never stopped telling our stories. At Amherst, I rejoiced at being in an environment where Du Bois's commitment to the education of African American people could be felt everywhere.

I spent many full days in the small study carrels of the library, studying Du Bois's papers and other works. I would go into the library early in the morning and lose myself in the research and materials from the shelves. I found such joy in reading autobiographical accounts of African Americans people who were students during the periods that followed emancipation through to the *Brown* decision (1865–1954), and also learning about the persistent efforts of African American people to obtain education across the decades. I still draw inspiration from all that Black people were able to accomplish in the incredibly productive twelve-year period of Reconstruction, when Black people were fully recognized and had the freedom to be elected to state legislatures. I learned about the work of Black legislators to make education free and accessible for all children—Black children and poor white children. And the great pride that they took in this work. I saw clearly how the people of my generation directly benefited from their accomplishments.

Reading of our history after the end of Reconstruction, I also saw how quickly the opportunities and possibilities for our people diminished with the emergence of Jim Crow, the brutality of the Klan, and the proliferation of laws that would entrap Black people in the South within the persistent power structures of white supremacy. This history documented the ups and downs of the struggles of Black people, the advances and the retractions, as the system revived old and manifested new methods of oppression. I began to see how this pattern issued forward into my lived experience and into the classrooms and schools where I had been and now found myself.

I was utterly transported by my research. I would emerge from the library in the evenings and blink as my eyes adjusted once again to the natural light of the sun going down on the day. I often had to shake my head to remember when and where I was. I would have been content to keep reading about this history of African American people, but Meyer Weinberg would urge me on in the writing of my dissertation saying, "Josie, you've done enough research. I'm going to lock you into a room until you finish the writing! You don't need to do any more research." But I found this immersion in the literature so essential. As I would write in my dissertation: "An historical review of these issues is necessary because the struggle is on-going and the obstacles to racial justice, political equity, and equal educational outcomes continue to persist today for Black people. . . . these historical events are important to know and discuss because the past helps us to determine the future."

During my studies, I also visited fourth-grade classrooms at a suburban school just outside Amherst. In the early 1980s, busing plans were being implemented in Massachusetts, and many Black students were being bussed from urban school districts, like Springfield, to predominantly white suburban schools. I observed that Springfield students arrived at this suburban school with clear differences in the levels of their academic preparedness, differences that neither the schools nor the teachers were prepared to admit or address. The teachers at the school had not had experience teaching African American students and rather than develop strategies for addressing the academic differences among the students, they permitted the African American students to try to downplay the scholastic differences using skillful expression and performance. While the teachers and other students enjoyed the "performances" of the Black students, I was reminded of how I used to watch Black boys in my community while growing up. Before the age of five, they would walk with their little shoulders back and with such confidence that they were a delight to observe. Then after a few years of attending school and being told what they could not do, their heads would bow. They seemed to lose confidence and bend over as they walked. It was as though, as the years passed, you could see the pride drain from them as they came to embody the expectations and stereotypes of the majority culture. I was eager to figure out how to restore the confidence to our Black students.

While I was studying at Amherst, James Baldwin was a visiting scholar at Hampshire College, just down the road. On one occasion, he came to our campus to give a lecture. Baldwin was one of my idols; I attended the lecture with great anticipation. I was struck by the calm, forceful confidence in his voice and message, and I was thrilled to be in his presence. He spoke with such authority about the value that African American people brought to this society and how important it was for Black people to write, think, and talk about our contributions to this country. I had a chance to visit and talk with him. His pride in his people was contagious and I found his words to be so very affirming.

Friends and family also visited Amherst during my studies there. Vice President Mondale came to campus while I was a student as part of his presidential campaign in 1984. I believe it was the first time he introduced the voters to Representative Geraldine Ferraro, his running mate and the first woman nominated for vice president by a major political party. Norrene had completed her master's degree in electrical engineering at Stanford and had taken a job at Lanier Business Products, a company with offices in Bedford, Massachusetts. Her work at the time focused on developing the code for Lanier's first digital voice messaging system. Periodically, she would spend weekends in Amherst with me, and we would go shopping at antique and flea markets. We enjoyed each other's company and our relationship deepened.

In February 1986, at the age of fifty-five, I received my doctor of education degree from the University of Massachusetts at Amherst. Patrice, Norrene, and Josie attended the ceremony and expressed their great pride and inspiration at my being the first in our family to get a doctor of education degree. Josie's husband at the time and their eight-month-old baby, Lauren Noelle, my first grandchild, were also there. I felt tremendous joy at having made a contribution to the literature on the role Black parents and the Black community played in providing education for our children and in amplifying the value that African Americans have placed on education throughout our history. Meyer wanted me to publish my dissertation. Unfortunately, I didn't follow through on this. Thirty years later, however, in 2016, my dissertation was digitized and made available online by the University of Massachusetts Libraries. To my great pride, my dissertation now shares the same home where the papers of W. E. B. Du Bois reside.

During the final year of my doctoral program, my beloved father had fallen ill: he had collapsed while at a dry cleaner with his wife, Martha. Doctors determined that he had had a mini-stroke. My dad and I were very close, even more so after my mother's death in 1960. Following his stroke, I spent time between Amherst and Houston in order to help care for him while completing my studies. My father and I spoke regularly every week, and during our conversations and my visits to Houston I could always count on hearing my father's observations of the politics and current events in the life of the city.

After the excitement of commencement ended and my daughters left, I returned to Houston to continue caring for Daddy and to think about what my next steps would be. My father continued to be a soft-spoken, quiet person, going about many of the daily habits and rituals as he always had. He would still get up every morning and stand watching himself in the bathroom mirror as he buttoned his shirt and tucked it into his pants, in exactly the way that I remembered seeing him dress when I was child. The family eventually hired a lady who came in the mornings to help Dad get ready for his day. When I was visiting, I would also help him to get dressed and ready in the mornings, even when the business of the day would involve the two of us just going to the front room to sit and talk.

Though my father was still engaged in some work with clients in his real estate business, as his faculties declined my brother Judson Jr. had stepped in to take over the majority of the activities of his business. My brother Jim and John Davis Jr., Martha's son, had a law practice that was also part of Judson W. Robinson and Sons. Dad would still banter with community members like he always had, but now after conversations he would ask one of us who the people were with whom he had engaged.

One day, my father set out on an errand to deliver some papers to one of his clients and was gone all day. Dad had always loved to be out and about driving around, but on this occasion he had said he would be right back. After several hours had passed, my brothers and I grew increasingly worried. Judson Jr. and Jim decided to go out looking for him and I stayed home, calling around to neighbors asking, "Have you seen Big Judson?" No one had seen him or knew where he was. As it grew later, we were beside ourselves. We didn't call the police: even as multigenerational Texans, we didn't have that kind of relationship with the police. Then suddenly, my father came back to the house on his own. He told us that he had been over by the Ship Channel, a great waterway in Houston. He had driven on the wrong side of a divided parkway and had gotten confused about where he was.

My father had always been very talented at doing things his way. There had been other minor incidents, such as when Dad had forgotten where he had parked the car, but nothing had so completely scared the family like this incident. Even though my father tried skillfully to make excuses for his getting lost, my brothers and I were terribly afraid that it would happen again, and we decided to take away his car keys. This was a terrible blow to my father and heartbreaking for me as well, because I knew what driving meant to his sense of independence. Even after my father was no longer permitted to drive, he would go out nearly every morning and clean the windshield of his car, just as he had done with the 1939 Lincoln he had driven when I was a child.

Daddy passed away on May 11, 1986, three months after my graduation. I was back in Nashville, at a meeting of the alumni association at Fisk, when I had gotten the call that he had suffered a heart attack. I returned to Houston immediately and joined Martha, her two children, and my brothers at the hospital, but he never recovered from the heart attack. We were all there as a family at my father's bedside when he died. The crowd overflowed the church at my father's funeral service and the number of cars in his funeral procession stretched for miles.

12

HOME TO MINNEAPOLIS

I BRIEFLY CONSIDERED staying in Houston after my brothers and I settled our father's affairs, but I think I always knew I would eventually return to Minneapolis. Even before Chuck and I had left for Denver in 1974, I was aware how I had become anchored there. I had spent so much time working in service to the Minneapolis community with so many wonderful and caring people, especially those who had been responsible for inviting me into this work when I had first arrived: Robert Williams, director of the Minneapolis Urban League; Matthew Little, president of the Minneapolis chapter of the NAACP; Alpha Smaby, who served two terms in the Minnesota House of Representatives; Florence Gray, who as president of the Minneapolis League of Women Voters engaged me in the organization; and Celia Logan, a colleague of Chuck's at Honeywell. All of these politically savvy women and men had helped me understand the political and social climate in Minnesota, which was deeply important to me.

I recognized that Minneapolis had become my home and that during the twelve years since Chuck and I left for Denver my deepest desire was to return to Minneapolis and revive the strong connections I had developed there. In fact, while I was in Amherst, I hung a note on my bedroom mirror that my dearest friend Mahmoud El-Kati had written, reassuring me that my friends would always welcome me back and that my study at Amherst was important to our community and our history. I read it daily.

After Daddy's affairs were settled, I left Houston and returned to Minneapolis. I stayed with my friend Pete Williams and his daughter Jennifer for a few days while my best friend, Katie McWatt, drove me around to find housing. We were dismayed yet slightly amused to see that we faced the same obstacles we had fought so hard against during our struggle to pass the Fair Housing Bill in 1961. Twenty-five years had passed, but time after time the properties that landlords had told me on the phone were available somehow weren't any longer when I arrived. Today as I write this book, I often find myself shaking my head in frustration because of the truth of the adage "The more things change, the more they remain the same." More and more, I realize that the lesson history has taught me is that the views the majority culture holds are so deeply etched into their fabric that no law we can pass will change them.

Thankfully, within only a few days after I began my search, I found apartments in two buildings in the Loring Park neighborhood. One of the apartments was on Groveland Avenue and the other was a block away on Groveland Terrace. When I went to sign the lease the next day, I discovered that for some reason I had mixed up the building on Groveland Terrace with Summit House, the building on Groveland Avenue. But I had already scheduled my flight back to Houston to begin the moving process and time was short—I needed to get to the airport. So I signed the lease at Summit House and thought I could move later if I needed to. I'm so glad I signed that lease. It turned out to be one of those times when you say, "God works in strange and mysterious ways." Summit House was where I was meant to be. I moved in 1985 and have been there ever since.

• • •

I remember visiting St. Peter Claver School when we moved to Minnesota in 1956. St. Peter Claver Catholic Church, a Roman Catholic parish in St. Paul, was founded in 1892 with the purpose and continuing mission to be a church for African American Catholics. The church welcomes all people of different backgrounds but draws a particular sense of connectedness to our African tradition, which has taught us resilience, faith in God, perseverance, and full participation in our worship and faith as Catholics. My memory includes a school with a few Black nuns; they were preparing to shut down the building because the school was closing and would not reopen. When I returned to Minneapolis, Father Kevin M. McDonough was the parish priest. I will always remember his greeting "Welcome home" as I entered the front door of the church my first time back in Minneapolis. Since that greeting, I have become more deeply involved in service to my church.

I also soon began reconnecting with friends and former colleagues in community organizations, foundations, and at the University of Minnesota to explore career opportunities that might be available to me, and to determine which opportunities stood out as something I would want to pursue long term. I have a vivid memory of discussing a job opportunity at lunch with a friend from one of the foundations that supported the work I was doing in the community before I left. I remember breaking out in a sweat while we were talking and feeling nervous and terribly embarrassed. All I could think was, "Oh my goodness, I'm sweating." I am sure he didn't realize what was happening; he probably didn't even notice. I'm equally sure that if I had been having lunch with a woman in my age group, we both would have understood and would probably have laughed, since in all probability we would both be experiencing what all women go through when we pass our childbearing years.

More to the point, however, as I talked with my foundation friend at lunch that day, I remembered being on committees that reviewed grant proposals and being troubled that funders did not seem to review what applicant groups stated in their mission; I recalled that funders did not always seem to care whether recipients were successful in meeting their stated goals with the funds they received. But nobody ever asked if the grantees met their objectives, at least not in the reviews that I had an opportunity to participate in. So I would wonder why those questions were not being asked, and whether the money awarded was really making a difference. I knew that my principal objective was to share the research and knowledge I had gained during my doctoral studies with my community, and I needed time to figure out where I would go in order to accomplish this. In the end, I didn't think working for a foundation would be the way to achieve my goal.

Meanwhile, I began spending more time with Pete and his family. Our families had been very close for many years. He and his wife, Lillian, were one of the couples in the group of friends Chuck and I got to know shortly after our arrival in Minneapolis. We spent lots of time together while our children were growing up, and Pete was one of the men in the group who worked with Chuck, Luther Prince, and several others to form the Monitors club, which provided African American men with financial investment skills and civic opportunities. Lillian was the first director of the university's Office of Equal Opportunity and Affirmative Action. I had been able to vote for her and for the position when I was on the Board of Regents.

Now Lillian had passed away, and Chuck and I were divorced. Convinced that it would be both natural and good for us to see more of each other, his daughter Pam began to arrange that. She convinced him to come to Amherst during my last months of study, to visit me on the pretense of a business trip. We had dinner together and reviewed our family and friendship history. I toured him around my campus and showed him homes and buildings that I knew would be of interest to him. Pete was an architect and had a great interest in seeing architectural structures wherever he traveled. In the Twin Cities, he was known as an architect for social justice and became the first Black president of the national American Institute of Architects (AIA). He was co-owner of Williams/O'Brien Associates, an architectural firm whose primary focus was urban renewal, developing properties that served lower-income residents. But Pete and his firm did not stop there: they involved community members who lived in the neighborhoods where they were planning to build housing developments. Pete was always concerned about people's living environment and made sure to include things that would make the residents' area pleasant, adding features such as gardens and parking spaces.

Pam was right. Pete and I were very compatible and ended up being close companions for the next twenty years. When we started dating, it was difficult for me to consider a new relationship—it felt unnatural. However, remembering Margaret Mead's article was as helpful to me then as it had been when I was trying to understand my divorce from Chuck. Considering her explanation of life's changes made it easier, and I was able to see that I was now experiencing a different phase of my life.

Our shared family and community experiences were there, and having known Pete and Lillian and their family for such a long time felt natural. However, the environment I shared with him was different. I had never experienced the social part of life that he and his family had. As a girl growing up, my family had never taken vacations or road trips. Galveston and the surrounding beaches were our greatest experience of vacation. Visits to see my grandmother in

San Antonio were our happiest moments. Therefore, I rarely thought about vacation. Pete's family loved camping out and going on skiing trips. He owned a boat and an airplane and his children enjoyed flying to Kentucky, the home state of Pete's mother, and they took other short trips here and there. These were all new experiences to me. In fact, I had never thought of those activities as anything I would consider as vacations. But when Pete and I began to date, or whatever my generation called it at that time, I found that I became interested in travel and vacation. Pete and I went to Hawaii five times during our years together. We continued going to social events with our mutual friends and seeing our children and grandchildren for birthday parties and Christmas celebrations.

Another interesting part of my relationship with Pete was that even though his work was very community oriented, his politics were conservative. We frequently went on long walks along the Mississippi River near his home on West River Parkway and often engaged in heated arguments about political matters. This proved to me that one could have a fulfilling personal relationship with someone whose political views are different from yours.

Sadly, Pete developed Alzheimer's. Pam moved him to her home in California so she could be with him during that stage of his life, and Pete lived with her until his death in 2011. Pam became interested in Alzheimer's patients during her time of caring for her father, taking courses in the care of dementia patients. She converted her home into a small, very nice facility for five to six patients. She named it Pete's Place and kept the facility for several years after Pete died.

After meeting with friends and colleagues in several fields, I decided that I could best share the learnings from my doctoral program at Amherst with the community through the University of Minnesota, expanding on the role I had played with Black parents before I left Minneapolis. My experience with the children in Massachusetts solidified the need I saw for us to do something to combat the stereotyping of our children, which was causing them to lose the bright light in their eyes before they even completed elementary school.

I was introduced to Dr. Sally McKee. Her husband, Dr. Michael McKee, had been a member of the Health Science Committee that I chaired during my tenure on the Board of Regents. Sally reconnected me with old and new College of Education faculty and administrators, and I was soon offered a senior fellow position in the College of Education.

I was eager to discuss my dissertation work with my colleagues and to continue making new discoveries. My dissertation had focused on the years 1865–1954, when Black parents clearly maintained the view of our ancestors that education was emancipation. I was eager to test what I thought was the continued cultural behavior of Black parents and community members in educating their children. Slaves were denied any form of education; in fact, they were punished if they tried to learn. However, they were determined to learn and were willing to suffer for that goal. I wanted our children to know this history of being committed to follow in the footsteps of their ancestors. Thankfully, I was given permission to develop Minneapolis Public School connections with parents and students in order to test methods of encouraging parent engagement to stimulate a stronger desire in our children to study and learn.

I created a community group that met weekly with hopes of gaining insight into whether Black parents, and Black adults in general, placed the same value on education in 1987 as Black parents did in the slave, emancipation, and Reconstruction eras. My colleagues and college administrators were also interested in learning. I recruited parents, teachers, and representatives from a broad cross-section of our community and designed questions for discussion that would lead us to

139

these insights. I was blessed to have as my assistant a student scholar, Carol McGee Johnson, who was working on her doctorate. Carol was from a prominent St. Paul family—her father was the first Black engineer at IBM's Rochester plant. Our committee met for a year, and I was convinced that parents in our community needed to be better equipped to be actively engaged in their children's schools and educations.

As we were completing the project, we learned that a foundation in New York was accepting proposals that would stimulate learning strategies in public schools. The name of the project was the Beacons. I had for several years thought about possible opportunities for creating a partnership between classroom teachers and directors of after-school programs. I thought they could collaborate on ways that after-school activities could reinforce classroom lessons. Unfortunately, teachers and other professionals felt that the academic training curriculum would be too difficult to implement. I couldn't accept the idea that something that could be so helpful to our children was deemed "too difficult," so I reached out and found a different partner. The Minneapolis YMCA was interested and believed along with me in the concept I was proposing, and so we applied for the grant explaining that the YMCA would be an ideal partner in lieu of the Minneapolis Public Schools. Fortunately, we were awarded the funding and Minneapolis YMCA was the grant recipient. I served on the staff selection committee and shared my thoughts with Doris Baylor, the creative director we hired. She was very interested in designing after-school programs that would encourage children to learn through play, for example, a program that used the math at grade level would be reinforced with play. Her determination allowed her to find ways to expand the concept; she was able to create a relationship with teachers and other school professionals. Over time, the program received many awards and positive modeling of teaching beyond the classroom.

Something else I wanted to do as a fellow in the College of Education was to find other ways to recruit more Black educators to teach in Minnesota's public schools. I designed a program that invited graduate students from historically Black colleges and universities to do advanced work at the University of Minnesota and to invite faculty from those institutions to be mentors to white faculty at the university, with the goal of teaching them better ways of working with students of color. We did enjoy some success with this project, and a few of the students we recruited began teaching in the Minneapolis and St. Paul schools after graduation. Unfortunately, the culture in Minnesota can be very closed and unwelcoming, which made it difficult for most of the teachers to stay here.

While my career was growing and thriving, so were my daughters in their varying fields of work and expertise. Josie graduated cum laude from Harvard and received her J.D. from Berkeley, became a member of the New York State Bar, and became senior executive vice president and chief diversity and inclusion officer at CBS. Norrene graduated with a dual degree from Spelman and Georgia Tech in engineering, and a master's degree in electrical engineering from Stanford. She started her own business, Red Bridge Organizational Change Management Consulting, and worked as a consultant to Delta Airlines; she continues to advise high-profile companies. Patrice rose to chief of staff for Texas Congressman Mickey Leland, chair of the U.S. Subcommittee on Hunger. I have great pride that my children are following in the tradition of our African American ancestors.

13

OUR PATRICE

MONDAY, AUGUST 7, 1989, is a day I will never forget. It was the day our family was changed forever and I lost my firstborn child.

I had been in a meeting with a colleague and the dean of the College of Education and Human Development on the Minneapolis campus. In this meeting, we were developing strategy for a partnership between historically Black colleges and universities in an effort to increase Black candidates for the public school teacher applications. I left the conference room at the end of the meeting and returned to my office. When I checked my phone messages, there was one from General Colin Powell. I couldn't imagine why General Powell would be calling me at this time of day. I returned his call right away, only to hear the most devastating news anyone could ever imagine receiving: he had called to tell me that a plane carrying Patrice and Congressman Mickey Leland had gone missing. As chief of staff to Congressman Leland, who was chair of the House Subcommittee on Hunger, Patrice was traveling with him and a delegation of fifteen on a government mission to bring relief to Sudanese refugees in the Fugnido refugee camp, which was located in a remote area in Ethiopia.

The rest of the day, and in fact the next period of my life, was confusing and sad. Chuck, Norrene, Josie, and I tried to keep up hope and relied heavily on our spiritual faith. We were blessed with the support and prayers of our family, friends, and all who knew Patrice.

During the search period, because Congressman Leland's trip to Africa was a government initiative mission, General Colin Powell became our family contact during the long search. The plane had vanished while attempting to fly through heavy rain, wind, and thunderstorms to its destination of Addis Ababa. He called every night to update Chuck and me; we had late-night conversations with him. We felt General Powell became personally involved in the search for the small plane.

My life became an unbelievable experience during those horrible seven days of waiting. As much as I tried to maintain a sense of normalcy, I could not. I tried to work but couldn't focus. I began to feel that I had died; it was as though I couldn't find myself. I started putting my personal things in neat stacks and keeping them in places where they could be easily found if I died. I saw Patrice in everything I did. I saw her as a young girl playing on the swings in her elementary schoolyard at the University of Minnesota, as a teenager, a college student, and as a grown woman. And I dreamed of her every night. In my dreams, she talked with me and tried to tell me not to worry. In one vivid dream, I saw her dressed in white, as though she were an angel, and she said, "Mom, I am okay. Don't worry." That experience will stay in my memory forever.

Chuck had returned to Minneapolis several years before this tragic event and was living in a condominium on Dean Boulevard, near Lake Calhoun (now Bde Maka Ska). We were at his home when General Powell called seven days after the plane was reported missing to tell us that the wreckage had been found. He gave us the official Pentagon report: "The plane had hit a mountain that was forty-three hundred feet above sea level, having missed clearing the peak by about three hundred feet. There were no survivors." They were only seventy-five miles from their destination. My precious child was gone, and all they were able to retrieve of her remains was her Seiko watch. I still have it, and I wear it every day.

I immediately left Chuck's home and went back to my place to call and talk with Josie and Norrene. Josie had received a call from an official person and already had the news when I called her. Over the next days and weeks, we received many lovely cards and messages from officials, both American and Ethiopian. That was meaningful to us.

Chuck and I were so proud when Patrice Yvonne was born. We were living in Cambridge, in student housing as Chuck was working on his graduate studies at Massachusetts Institute of Technology. We had the good fortune of giving birth to Patrice on June 2, 1954, in a hospital in Worcester. How could we possibly know that we would lose her two months after her thirty-fifth birthday, causing us the most profound grief a family could ever endure?

We knew early that Patrice had much promise and that she would eventually continue our family legacy of a dedication to service to the Black community. Over her short life, she proved our perception to be true. This was evident when she was a small child, by the way she helped with her two younger sisters and in the care she showed her friends throughout elementary, middle, and high school. At a very young age, she became the friend to go to for advice and counsel. After her death, I found many notes from her friends in a small trunk, thanking her for listening and for helping them solve a problem. She loved theater and dance, and during the summer months she volunteered for park and recreation activities in our Bloomington community.

Though we lived in Bloomington when she entered Abraham Lincoln High School, she and her sisters joined me during my community engagement activities and were able to know the places and people I worked with. The girls knew staff and volunteers at The Way and Wheatley House in North Minneapolis. Chuck and I included our girls in our interest and community efforts.

I will never forget the day Patrice came home from school upset. "Mother, you won't believe this!" she exclaimed. She told me that her school was gearing up for a big game, probably football. I don't remember what school they were going to play, but in her school's entryway there was a poster of an Indian head along with the words "Massacre the Mohawks." Patrice wanted to make the school aware of this racism and to request that the poster be taken down, and she asked me to accompany her. I was proud of her desire to create change and went back to the school with her to support her. She eloquently presented her argument to the principal, teachers, coaches, and others in the principal's office. Her effort didn't have an effect at that time: the poster stayed up and the game went on. Many years later, racism in the athletic world depicting negative images of Native Americans became a national issue. Public schools, college programs, and professional organizations have indeed become more sensitive. Looking back, I can see very clearly that she showed great awareness and sensitivity before it became a broader issue. She became class president in her junior year at Abraham Lincoln.

Like her father and me, Patrice went to Fisk, where she graduated summa cum laude in 1976, with a double major in political science and public administration. She was junior class president and a member of Who's Who in American Schools and Colleges. She achieved membership in the Gold Key and Phi Beta Kappa national honor societies and was elected president of the Fisk student body. For her college internship in 1974–75, she worked for Representative Alvin King of the General Assembly of Tennessee.

Upon graduation from Fisk, and with a recommendation from John Hope Franklin, Patrice was accepted to a joint degree program at the Woodrow Wilson School of Public Affairs at Princeton University. There she studied urban and domestic policies. She was a Root-Tilde Scholar and received her law degree from New York University and a master's degree in public administration at Princeton in 1980. During that graduate study period, she served as an intern for Vice President Mondale.

After graduating from law school, Patrice moved to Houston and began her life of public service as a law clerk for U.S. District Court Judge Gabrielle K. McDonald, the first Black person to be appointed by President Carter to U.S. District Court for the Southern District of Texas. When she completed her clerkship, she joined the law firm of Mayor, Day, and Caldwell. There, she continued our family's legacy of dedication to public interest and civil rights. Patrice participated in the National Urban League's first Class of Trustees Under Age Thirty and was once arrested along with others during a civil rights protest. On a pro bono basis, she coordinated the culmination of the *Delores Ross v. Houston Independent School District,* a case that had its start with *Brown v. Board of Education,* the year Patrice was born. She settled it twenty-eight years later, drafting a settlement agreement that mandated the Houston Independent School District to be racially desegregated. Until this day, the agreement continues to be the monitoring document for that district's compliance.

Congressman Leland was a family friend, and Patrice often helped out in his Houston office. She joined his staff, and in 1987, he promoted her to join him in Washington, D.C., to become his legislative director. In this position, she concentrated on issues addressing the telecommunications arena. She was a tenacious negotiator. For the congressman she drafted legislation dealing with increased opportunities for Black people in media ownership and employment. In

January 1989, Patrice was promoted to chief of staff of Congressman Leland's Washington and Houston offices. She worked closely with his initiatives on the energy, health, and communications committees on which he served and on the Committee on Hunger, which he created and chaired. It was the pursuit of the goals of this select committee, to help eradicate the insidious problem of world hunger, that took Patrice to Ethiopia on August 7, 1989, where she surrendered her life, striving as always to serve. Her tombstone reads, "And she served."

We held her funeral service at Zion Baptist Church in Minneapolis. Zion's pastors, Reverend Curtis Herron and Reverend William (Bill) Smith, officiated and spoke at the funeral. She is buried at Lakewood Cemetery near the condominium where her beloved father lived. Multiple services were held in Minneapolis and Houston to honor Patrice and Congressman Mickey Leland. Among those who came to pay their respects were Congressman Leland's pregnant widow, Alison, and his mother, Alice Rains; his press secretary, Alma Newsom; and most of his staff. Also attending were Kathy Whitmire, the first woman mayor of Houston along with several members of Houston's city council; Atlanta mayor Andrew Young; U.S. Representatives Gary Ackerman (D–New York), Al Wheat (D–Missouri), Ron Dellums (D–California and chairman of the Congressional Black Caucus), and Harold Ford (D–Tennessee). Dellums's aide Joyce Francine Williams, an expert on child health and nutrition issues, was among those killed in the crash.

We will always miss our dear Patrice. Her sisters will always speak fondly of her. When talking about her to the African American Registry, Josie said, "She was an inspirational role model who led the way with humor and insight well beyond her years."

14

THE EASTCLIFF
GATHERING

MY ONGOING WORK AT THE UNIVERSITY helped to pull me through my grief at the loss of my daughter. On campus, African American students were continuing the struggle of the 1960s with special events that recognized progress and yet called attention to work still to be done. Activities during the commemoration of Dr. Martin Luther King Jr.'s birthday and Black history month had become important expressions of agency for African American students on campus. Through efforts made by myself and others, university student groups were able to sponsor events and speakers, and they had the freedom to decide who they would feature.

In the first years after my return to Minneapolis, between 1988 and 1990, the Africana group presented three controversial speakers: Minister Louis Farrakhan, leader of the Nation of Islam; Steve Cokely, aide to former Chicago Mayor Eugene Sawyer; and Kwame Ture (formerly known as Stokely Carmichael), the past prime minister of the Black Panther Party. The students' primary motivations were to expand their political education and provide the community with opportunities to hear voices that were outside of conventional names connected to the civil rights movement. Little did we know how these choices would become fuel for a great animosity between Blacks and Jews in the university community.

The Africana student group brought in Farrakhan in May 1988. Inspired by his strong message of Black pride, independence, and economic power, the students believed his visit would be tremendously empowering to the Black community, both on and off campus. However, offensive and anti-Semitic remarks he had made in recent years caused the Jewish Community Relations Council/Anti-Defamation League of Minnesota and the Dakotas to protest. My friend Mahmoud El-Kati recalled a meeting with members of the Jewish community, which included rabbis, students, parents, and citizens at large who demanded that the Africana group be persuaded to cancel Farrakhan's visit. Their attempts did not succeed.

Some two thousand individuals attended Farrakhan's talk, and security, which included metal detectors and searches of personal property, was unusually tight. Farrakhan was more than an hour late, but when he stepped out onto the stage surrounded by eight bodyguards the audience erupted in cheers and resounding applause. The next day, the *Minneapolis Star Tribune* reported that while "a small entourage of picketers protested outside the auditorium, Farrakhan captivated the unexpectedly large audience using humor to incite the crowd with his messages on politics, racism and religion."

The following year the student group sponsored a speech by Steve Cokely. His visit was not well received by either the university or outside community—nor were his views that Jewish doctors used the HIV/AIDS virus as an attempt to commit genocide against Africans. His visit further enraged the Jewish community.

And finally, in 1990, the group featured Kwame Ture as part of its Africana History Month lecture series. During his talk, titled "Zionism: White Supremacy, Imperialism, or Both?" Ture stated that Judaism as a religion must be respected. However, he denounced the political philosophy of Zionism, the modern movement calling for the return to a Jewish national home, saying that "Zionism should be destroyed" and charging that some Zionists worked hand in hand with the Nazis during World War II to strengthen sentiment for a Jewish homeland.

150

Ture's speech was the last straw for the Jewish community. At this point, the Jewish Community Relations Council/ Anti-Defamation League of Minnesota and the Dakotas requested a meeting with University President Nils Hasselmo. An article published in the *Star Tribune* following Ture's speech stated that Morton Ryweck, then executive director of the group, asked President Hasselmo "to criticize bigoted incidents or speakers that come to the campus." Ryweck also invited President Hasselmo to view a tape of the speech.

After viewing the tape, President Hasselmo met with members of the Africana group. He explained his vision of unity with diversity, a concept that meant that we all must listen to and learn from each other in order to make the university a safe, equitable, accessible institution for all—students, staff, and faculty. "We want to protect freedom of speech and your right to bring in who you want to bring in and we will protect that right," he said. "But we must take whatever steps we can to minimize further these flare-ups of racial divisiveness before it turns into violence." The group of students saw this comment as one more in a long line of attempts to stifle free speech and academic freedom at the university. The students then challenged pro–Zionist organizations to view the tape of Ture's speech during five scheduled showings and to debate its contents. Citing Ture's comment that Judaism as a religion must be respected, the group wanted to clarify that any debate they had was with Zionists and not with those who adhere to the Jewish religion.

Concern about relations between the Black and Jewish communities, coupled with his attitude of justice and fairness, led President Hasselmo to invite me to a meeting he had called with African American university personnel and a group of Jewish citizens. Nils and I had worked together on a number of projects throughout my years as senior fellow in both the College of Education and the Hubert H. Humphrey Institute (now the Humphrey School of Public Affairs), and he was very much aware of my conviction that Blacks and Jews have often been close because of the commonality of our issues. He wanted to find a way to heal relations between our two communities and was confident that I could help to find a way to accomplish that healing. Members of the Black Student Cultural Center and the Jewish Community Relations Council had agreed to form a Black–Jewish student group, but Hasselmo felt that the situation was still potentially volatile. I was thrilled with everyone's willingness to discuss the issues—it was my dream that our two communities could continue to come together, as there was still much more to be done. I planned a second gathering and invited Black and Jewish faculty to talk together. I asked Hy Berman to work with me to recruit Jewish faculty. Dr. Berman was the first Jewish professor hired by the university and was highly respected by Jews at the school and in the community. His invitation would surely be taken seriously.

We thought an off-campus location—a warm and cozy environment with refreshments—would encourage connection and allow for discussion of the delicate issues of freedom of speech for African American students, their choice of speakers, and the Jewish community's feelings. President Hasselmo kindly offered Eastcliff, the off-campus manor that serves as both the president's residence and a gathering space for the university community.

Dr. Berman and I were pleased that some twenty faculty, staff, and students attended the late-afternoon gathering. The winter sun streamed through the large windows of the beautiful living room as though blessing this event, the first ever meeting of the University of Minnesota's Black and Jewish communities. And as daylight turned to dusk, the lively discussion we had hoped for took place.

Everyone felt comfortable enough to share their thoughts and feelings. Jewish attendees were outraged by Kwame Ture's views on Zionism and found Minister Farrakhan's characterization of Judaism as a "gutter religion" and Israel as "a wicked hypocrisy" extremely offensive. To make matters worse, Farrakhan's speech was held on an important Jewish holiday, Shavuot, the day that marks the establishment of the covenant at Sinai between God and Israel and the revelation of the Ten Commandments. The African Americans explained that they understood why the student group believed Farrakhan and Kwame Ture were appropriate speakers for the university. Black students felt inspired and empowered by the messages these men offered and believed that the large audiences they generated were proof that many Blacks both at the university and in the community at large also considered them important figures. Further, the students explained that rather than calling Judaism itself a "dirty religion," Farrakhan was referring to how some have used it to do dirty work. They pointed out that his speech also lashed out at Christians and Muslims for their hypocrisy; they reiterated that though Ture denounced Zionism, he defended Judaism as a religion that must be respected. By the end of the discussion, we all believed we had made significant strides in repairing the rift that had occurred as a result of having these speakers.

One of the early outcomes of the Eastcliff gathering was that Rose Brewer, chair of African American Studies, and Riv-Ellen Prell, a Jewish associate professor in the Department of American Studies, developed and team-taught an experimental course that they offered in the women's studies program. It was a powerful course designed to look at the historical roles and patterns that had evolved among African American and Jewish people in America.

Pleased as I was with the restoration of the relationships, my thoughts moved far beyond what was accomplished that day. I had been involved with the university for thirty-two years at that point and was very familiar with how the politics and attempts to achieve diversity in terms of race, color, ethnicity, and cultural orientation had evolved over time, even before the mid-1950s, when I first set foot on campus. When I looked back, it was clear that time and again committees and task forces had been formed, studies had been conducted, and reports with recommendations had been written in efforts to bring about change. A few good examples were the commitment made in 1969 to increase access for African Americans through scholarships, counseling, and advising; similar commitments to Chicano students in 1970; and the development of the African American Studies Department following the 1969 Black student occupation of Morrill Hall.

There was also the twenty-one-member Minority Advisory Committee that President Kenneth Keller appointed in 1985, which Nils Hasselmo continued when he became president. Initially, the Minority Advisory Committee met four times a year and adopted these two central purposes: to involve community groups in monitoring progress and achieving specific goals to strengthen diversity; and to enlist community support in the university's state and national legislative efforts to increase resources for students and faculty of color. However, shortly after its inception, President Keller gave them the additional task of preparing an in-depth response to the recommendations to the *Commitment to Focus,* a project instituted by the Higher Education Coordinating Board.

In May 1987, the Minority Advisory Committee, chaired by Dr. John Taborn, associate professor of African American studies and psychology, submitted its *Final Report of the Special Committee on Minority Programs in Support of Commitment to Focus.* In the report, commonly known as the *Taborn Report,* the task force offered twenty-two detailed recommendations, some of which included: to expand minority student and faculty recruitment and retention efforts; to create staff

154

development plans and graduate education for minorities; to engage majority faculty and staff in courses and programs to upgrade their awareness, understanding, and communication skills with minority students; to provide the Office of Equal Opportunity with an associate dean to develop and implement initiatives for recruitment, retention, and graduation of minority undergraduate and graduate students; and to fund the implementation of the recommendations. Attempts were made to implement those recommendations, including making academic and counseling programs available to minority middle and high school students; creating research stipends that allowed minority students to work on research topics of their choice; and founding the Bridge Fund program, which provided funding for recruitment and appointment of faculty of color.

In looking back across the history of the university, it was very clear to me that, on the one hand, a historical pattern of intolerant behavior existed, and on the other, there was a history of sincere efforts to address those behaviors. But earnest as the efforts were, they only had had limited success. I believed that something different needed to be done.

My key feeling was that as a research institution based in the middle of a major city, this university had both a unique opportunity and a responsibility to respond to the academic and social needs of our state in solid and lasting ways. My vision had always been of a university that recognized and honored the value of the town/gown relationship—in other words, a university that utilized the skills of its faculty, its students, its location, and its research to respond to troubling issues that needed to be addressed in our community. Such issues included the academic gap between majority and minority students in the public schools, minority health challenges, and the need to review government policies that negatively impacted the quality of life for Minnesota citizens. I wanted diversity to be integrated into the total system of the university's funding, promotion, hiring, recruitment, and retention of faculty, staff, and students.

In my report to President Hasselmo that followed our Eastcliff gathering, I declared my belief that in order to achieve his vision of unity with diversity, we must look beyond the university's African American and Jewish communities. The discussions that had taken place among Black and Jewish faculty, staff, and students provided the university with a unique window of opportunity to create a new paradigm that I believed could fulfill the president's commitment to encouraging and promoting an environment that respected cultural differences and enhanced full participation of all members of the university community. The important information we gleaned from the two groups caused me to believe we could learn even more from other minority groups—Native American, Chicano/Latino, and Asian faculty, staff, and students.

I didn't believe we could continue down the same path as the past, however. We needed to intentionally adopt a new approach. Also, though we needed to find out how other minority groups within the university community viewed us, we couldn't stop there. We needed to reach out beyond our ivory tower and take the risk of learning how we were seen by individuals outside of the university. Then, armed with solid information, we could develop projects and programs that were far more likely to effect lasting change. With that in mind, my report to President Hasselmo and his cabinet included a proposal for the development of an African American–Jewish Relations conference and for an all-university forum on diversity to explore the causes of the conflicts. I believed that without efforts to address the reasons why these issues were emerging, our university would be at risk for ongoing problems.

My research methods as a senior fellow in the College of Education and the Humphrey Institute included conducting meetings with community members, such as educators and parents, to get their input on how the university could help them achieve better educational outcomes—and to mentor them toward more positive parenting skills and achievement of stronger educational outcomes. My proposal included expanding this town/gown–gown/town approach to help us find out how other groups viewed us. Those groups would include legislators, local officials, educators, the media, people from various communities of color, the arts, and other segments of society.

15

DIVERSITY
AND THE UNIVERSITY

PRESIDENT HASSELMO embraced my proposal for a project that would move the university toward a partnership with the community and culminate in a forum on diversity, scheduled to take place in the spring of 1991. He committed the university to improving and enriching relationships among groups and expressed particular interest in community activities that would address issues of racial conflict and bigotry. To continue my work, he assigned me to the Office for Multicultural and Academic Affairs to develop the project.

My first step was to conduct a qualitative study that consisted of interviews with university faculty, staff, students, and administrators with the purpose of hearing their views on issues of intolerance that persisted on campus: intolerance for religious, racial, cultural, and lifestyle differences. I sought out and was generously provided with the names of individuals at the university who were members of the African American, Jewish, Native American, Asian, and Hispanic/Latino communities. By then, the early 1990s, the university had broadened its definition of diversity to include disabled individuals and members of the gay community, so we sought out their input as well. Informal meetings with each group were held over breakfast, and attendees were encouraged to consider some of the following questions:

- How do you think we should proceed in our efforts to deal with issues related to diversity and pluralism?

- In your opinion, what features of the University of Minnesota's environment are most important in contributing to the success of diversity?

- What have been your experiences in dealing with the issue of diversity?

- Have there been any particular individuals who have been especially helpful?

My team—students led by graduate consultant Nuri Hassumani—and I focused on these questions because we were aware of their importance to the people who participated in the study. We also knew that concerns related to diversity—racism, equal opportunity, conducive work environments, and the valuing of diverse lifestyles and cultures—are often relegated to the realm of private anxiety or brought up in the safe environment of family or close friends, who are often not in a position to do much more than listen.

Upon completion of my research, the first ever All-University Forum on Diversity was held on May 29, 1991, at the Earle Brown Continuing Education Center on the St. Paul campus. Its purpose was to begin discussing how we, as members of an institution of higher learning, could best address President Hasselmo's vision of unity with diversity. We designed the forum in a fashion that we hoped would pull in a good number of people from the communities who participated in our study. In order to accomplish this, we decided to create an event that would be entertaining and dramatic, an event we hoped would set a stage for an environment of trust so that we could get a sense of where we were at that time and where to go from here.

We were pleased that some 450 faculty, staff, administrators, and students attended the event on the Twin Cities campus, and others attended simulcasts on the Duluth, Crookston, Morris, and Waseca campuses. It was a lovely afternoon consisting of a keynote address by President Hasselmo; stories presented by a multicultural group of faculty, staff, and students; and Native American music performed by African American singer Faye Washington and a group of Native musicians.

I then shared my findings from the study we had conducted. There were three general types of statements made by the interviewees when they discussed the commitment of the university to the issue of diversity: (a) President Hasselmo's sincere commitment to diversity issues; (b) a general lack of commitment by the faculty and staff; and (c) statements of hope about the university instilling a sense of commitment in everyone regarding issues related to diversity. Interviews with faculty, administrators, and students illustrated the work still to be done. One faculty member said:

> I could have left the university and it wouldn't
> really have mattered to anybody. If the university
> is really supporting diversity, somehow it ought
> to find ways to keep people like me around.
> They have soft money for certain trial positions
> in the area of diversity. Nobody supports their
> research, understands it. They don't get tenure
> in departments. I think it's a farce. So when the
> university says it supports diversity, I say, let me
> see your behavior. Something needs to be done
> to locate the pockets of diversity and nurture them,
> support them. The university needs to take a hard
> look at itself and do some preventative work instead
> of always Band-Aid work.

A senior administrator said:

160 What am I most optimistic and most pessimistic
about in terms of this institution? Optimistic about
the fact that it is still positioned at a point where
it can do things that other institutions can't do.
We have not lost our options. Our back is not to
the wall. Minnesota isn't there yet. I'm pessimistic
because I see the same patterns emerging here,
and I'm fearful that we won't recognize that our
window of opportunity is very narrow. This is true
in terms of the university, and the Twin Cities as
a whole.

From a student:

I was attending college while still in high school.
I was a National Merit Scholar. I was admitted
directly to the Institute of Technology. One day
I went into a departmental office in IT. A staff
person said to me, "Looking for General College?
It's over there." People assumed I was in General
College. On another occasion I asked a professor for
more time on an assignment. He responded, "You
shouldn't be here if you can't keep up like everyone
else." I said, "My grades are good and I have a
scholarship." Then he said, "If you are so good,
you shouldn't need more time." Something totally
beyond my control had occurred. That professor
assumed I didn't have the ability and that I didn't
possess the drive.

One time I had a problem with a director of a
dorm. I filed a complaint and the director filed a
complaint. At the hearing, my complaint did not
appear. But the director's complaint did. They
decided in the director's favor.

Another interviewee stated:

> An international student with a disability had a
> wheelchair and limited use of his arms. At a final for
> one of his courses, there were a lot of calculations.
> There was no table, just chairs with tables attached.
> There was no place for him to pull up. He took a
> three-hour final on his lap trying to juggle things.
> He didn't finish the exam. The faculty member
> couldn't understand that this student didn't have
> equal access to the test.

President Hasselmo then led a discussion on the question "Where do we go from here?" In addressing that question, I made the audience aware that this forum was only the beginning. Plans were underway to expand the discussion to individuals and groups outside of the university community, some who were in attendance that day. We wanted to take an even larger look at the views of the external community in order to find out if we were fulfilling our obligations to address issues in the surrounding community and how we were doing in terms of the town/gown relationships. Attendees were left with the knowledge that the forum would continue in May 1992 with a formal presentation of the findings of our study and the research we would continue over the following year.

I left the Earle Brown Center that day with a sense that the strong attendance and positive reception to all that was presented were powerful indicators of the conviction President Hasselmo and I shared—that the responsibility for carrying forward our diversity initiatives rested on the shoulders of each member of the university community.

I was eager to begin planning the second forum. I was intent on keeping the promises I had made to the individuals who attended the first year: to present a formal report on the study my team and I had conducted, and to expand the study by capturing the thoughts and feelings of individuals outside the university community. As a fellow in the Humphrey Institute of Public Policy and Affairs, I had crossed paths with many people in various sectors of the community: legislators, local officials, educators, the media, people from the various communities of color, the arts, and other segments of society. I hosted a number of breakfast conversations with individuals from those sectors. It was my belief that those meetings would present an opportunity to make specific and clear recommendations to the university administration and then to translate them into policy through the regents. Indeed, I got quite an earful from individuals who attended these meetings. One thing I learned was that there was quite a disparity in the way that whites and minorities viewed the issue of diversity and pluralism at the university.

The 1992 forum also included Faye Washington's lovely music and addresses by President Hasselmo; Ettore "Jim" Infante, senior vice president for Academic Affairs and Provost; John Taborn; and several staff members and students. Representatives of the town/gown dialogue sessions also spoke, as well as members of the Minnesota Department of Civil Rights, the Minneapolis City Council, a state representative, and a representative of the media and educators. We continued to offer lectures, forums, seminars, and other events in the fall quarter of 1992, and in May 1993, we held a third forum. This final installment of the All-University Forum on Diversity was held on the Duluth campus and focused entirely on students. Mahmoud El-Kati was the keynote speaker.

I presented my *Report on the Self-Reflective Study: Attending to Human Details* in May 1992 at the Earle Brown Center to an attentive audience and a positive representation of the university and the community. Leading up to the event, I had developed a series of more than a hundred spring quarter events in response to the university community's desire for increased information on diversity issues. Lectures, forums, seminars, and other events developed by professors, artists, musicians, and others from minority communities, both local and national, were presented at all of our campuses. Noam Chomsky lectured on the "The Columbian Era: The Next Phase." The poet Sonia Sanchez gave a reading, and Debbie Stumblingbear gave a talk on Native American culture. Diversity roundtables were conducted and a weekly colloquium for professors and teaching assistants was held to teach them alternative teaching approaches for enhancing diversity in the university classroom.

My report was an in-depth reflection of the views of the one hundred students, staff, faculty, administrators, and community members interviewed by graduate students; it revealed how we at the University of Minnesota felt about how we were doing in terms of diversity. As pointed out in the examples above, many respondents indicated that making diversity and pluralism a reality would require making the institution more inclusive of minorities with regard to diversifying its student profile, having a greater number of minorities in the composition of its faculty and staff, and establishing a curriculum representative of the pluralistic nature of American society. They emphasized how important it was for President Hasselmo to provide the leadership necessary to bring about such fundamental changes in the values, goals, and objectives of the university.

Respondents also suggested strategies for making these changes and pointed out that, first and foremost, the quest for diversity and pluralism must be understood, supported, and catalyzed by those who are in key administrative positions—provosts, vice presidents, deans, department heads, and directors. In addition, they felt that while societal values and norms have a considerable influence on the manner in which the university's culture is shaped, administrators cannot wait for

164

future social or political forces to alter the values and culture of the university. Many interviewees believed that the administration and the regents were sincere in their commitment to diversity as a needed component of excellence but were skeptical that the university could or would deliver, as similar goals had been stated in past years. The issuing of memorandums and letters of intent for the promotion of diversity and pluralism was no longer considered adequate. To achieve the necessary changes, respondents believed that administrators would have to provide bold and visionary leadership.

Interestingly, the participants believed that efforts to achieve greater diversity and pluralism would be resisted by those whose support would be necessary. They believed, therefore, that the changes would come too slowly for some and perhaps too quickly for others. They cited the various complexities and contradictions inherent in the culture of the university, such as the pattern of intolerant behavior that I cited earlier, along with sincere efforts to address those behaviors as major issues in need of consideration and attention.

16

A NEW APPOINTMENT, THE SAME MISSION

ONE DAY EARLY IN THE FALL of 1992, Jim Infante invited me to meet with him and the other members of President Hasselmo's cabinet. We had worked together for a number of years on issues of diversity, among other things. Jim had a very informal manner overall, and it was not unusual for him to launch right into whatever he wanted to discuss. "Josie," he said, "as you know, we have spent an inordinate amount of time seeking the right person to fill the position of Associate Vice President for Academic Affairs and Associate Provost with Special Responsibility for Minority Affairs for the Office for Multicultural and Academic Affairs."

I couldn't agree more. The first person we hired for the position had left two years prior. Initially, we estimated that it would take a year to fill the position, but by the end of the first year no credible candidates had been found. A second search, which lasted another year, had yielded two viable candidates, but the top candidate was unable to accept due to health reasons, and the second choice candidate declined, citing Minnesota weather as the reason. We then offered the position to a faculty member, who elected to remain on the scholarly path rather than to switch to an administrative post.

When Jim approached me that day, I was prepared to engage in a discussion of ways we could expedite the search and get someone into the position as quickly as possible, but what Jim said next caught me by surprise: "Josie, the administrators decided to opt for the university's 'target of opportunity' provision," a provision that allows a position to be filled from outside a search committee's pool of candidates. He looked me sincerely and said, "We have decided to invite you to fill the post."

I had not applied for the position, nor had I expressed an interest in it. My hands were full managing the university-wide diversity forums and working with my team to find ways to implement the plan that had resulted from those forums. But Jim gently twisted my arm, asking if I would consider taking the position for a limited period of time. Before I could respond, Dennis Cabral, who had been serving in the position in an interim capacity, said, "Josie, it's a natural that you should fill the position. After all, you are the one who knows it best. You created this office and the position, and you have instilled within the university a more comprehensive view on diversity, not to mention that you have been connected with the university for a long time, even served as the first African American on the Board of Regents."

I needed to think hard about this, so I asked for time to mull it over. "Yes, of course," said Jim as he helped me on with my coat, then patted me on my shoulder. He opened the door for me and said once more, "Take all the time you need. But we are confident that you are the right person for this position."

My first thought as I walked back across campus to my office was that if I took the position, I would need to turn my diversity work over to someone else. I talked it over with members of the cabinet and the Board of Regents, as well as members of my team. Several of the people I worked closely with, including President Hasselmo and Robert Jones, who had worked side by side with me to develop and name the post, reminded me why we had created the position in the first place. We wanted the position to have power, voice, respect, and authority to implement diversity at the Associate Vice President for Academic Affairs level. The university had a well-established office to address the issues of equal opportunity and affirmative action. This new office would be sensitive to and focused on the recruitment and retention of faculty and students. Faculty would be assured of advancement and promotion in their scholarship, and students would receive mentoring and support for being successful at the university. We believed the position should include budget discussions with deans, department chairs, and recruiters. We felt that these steps would strengthen diversity on campus. Enlisting community support in the university's state and national legislative efforts to increase resources for students and faculty of color was an important strategy in the diversity plans.

Looking at it through that lens gave me a different perspective. I realized that in this role I would be in an even stronger position to implement the complex changes that need to take place in order to make the University of Minnesota a more diverse institution. Because of my deep respect for the university, the administration's commitment to diversity issues, and the Board of Regents' encouragement, I agreed to a three-year appointment, making it very clear that at the end of that time I would assess my strengths and progress to see if I should continue in the position. In October 1992, I was officially appointed.

On my first day in my new position, I spent a few moments at my desk reflecting on my relationship with the university and on what I hoped to accomplish in the three years I had agreed to serve in this capacity. By then, my relationship with the university had spanned some four decades. I gave birth to my youngest daughter here in Minneapolis and through the years was very involved in my three daughters' education, which began at the university's preschool and elementary school. I will forever mourn my first-born, Patrice, whose tragic death occurred when I was a senior fellow at the university in the College of Education.

Indeed, all my many years and positions held at the university led to this day. Now I sat behind the executive desk in the new suite of offices that the Office of Multicultural and Academic Affairs had recently been granted, overlooking the beautiful and lively Northrop Plaza. I was grateful for the many connections I made both within the academy and in the community, and for their trust in me to fulfill the mission of my newest and most important role at the University of Minnesota.

As associate vice president for academic affairs, I had system-wide jurisdiction over all academic matters pertaining to students and faculty of color as well as overall diversity issues. In my capacity of associate provost, I was responsible for academic affairs on the Twin Cities campus. I would serve on the president's cabinet and the provost's council and would participate in the Twin Cities deans' meetings to create ongoing communication with all of the vice presidents. I would work through the vice presidents to reach their deans. My hope was that this work would result in a different direction and organizational structure to produce institutional change.

After discussions over many years, I was eager to fulfill our initiative to infuse diversity and pluralism throughout the systems of the university—policy, planning, research, teaching, curriculum, and student services—and to link, inform, and encourage the various efforts that were being made with regard to the issue of diversity in the external communities served by the university. My work on the All-University Diversity Forum had shown me that people on and off campus were frustrated by what seemed to be an endless array of reports, statistics, and recommendations. President Hasselmo and I agreed that it was time for something new, a new paradigm of, as Nils put it, "action, action, action."

My first order of business was to complete one more analysis, which upon approval of the regents would allow us to move toward solid action. My report, titled *A New Paradigm: Evaluation for Effectiveness,* was an evaluation of what had been recommended and what had been tested under the direction of the first associate vice president. "Where have we spent resources?" I queried, and "What programs have been initiated that are designed to recruit and retain faculty and students of color? What has worked and what hasn't worked?" The mission of the Office for Multicultural and Academic Affairs was to make recommended programs work. Therefore, it was of primary concern that I identify issues related to that mission and our stated objectives and then to set forth strategies to achieve those objectives.

The report also outlined my mission and vision, and the action steps I wanted in order for the office to develop programs for staff and faculty of color, develop a clearinghouse for diversity, and continue the All-University Forum on Diversity. My plan indicated a shift from the first associate vice president, Delores Cross, whose focus had been on K–12 initiatives; I would instead focus on the university's students and the need to effect change within the institution before taking on such challenges as K–12 outreach.

Once my report was approved, I began a search for a strong staff of individuals who would create and maintain stability within the office. My first appointee was Presidential Scholar Robert Jones, an agronomist whose research focused on crop physiology, working specifically with maize. Dr. Jones is an internationally respected scholar whose work is steeped in research and outcomes. He is recognized worldwide for solving some of the critical issues of hunger and had been an academic and scientific consultant to Archbishop Desmond Tutu's South African Education Program. He was also an activist and top-notch administrator who shared my deep concern about diversity at the university and understood the budgeting process. We had worked together to develop the Office for Multicultural and Academic Affairs and had created the title of Associate Vice President for Academic Affairs and Associate Provost with Special Responsibility for Minority Affairs.

Back then, university staff and faculty could spend up to 49 percent of their time in other university positions, if they so desired. Dr. Jones was still very much involved in research and teaching, and I believed that the respect the institution had for him as a scholar coupled with his unique ability to listen and to hear what was being said would enable him to work on an equal basis with the deans across the university community. He accepted my offer to spend 49 percent of his time as director of faculty affairs. His charge was to assist me in my effort to raise the campus climate around diversity; to help me shape what was needed to move things to action based on his knowledge of the diversity scene for faculty, staff, and students; and to help the university test its goal of achieving diversity. The staff was a diverse group of wonderfully dedicated and supportive men and women who served in a variety of positions ranging from full-time employment to graduate assistants.

Prior to my appointment, I had worked with President Hasselmo to establish six minority advisory committees. I believed this to be an important step based on information gleaned from interviews with staff, faculty, and administrators during the *Self-Reflective Study.* The six groups were the University of Minnesota–Duluth American Indian Advisory Committee, the University of Minnesota–Morris American Indian Advisory Committee, the Twin Cities American

Indian Advisory Committee, the African American Advisory Committee, the Asian American and Pacific Islander Advisory Committee, and the Chicano/Latino Advisory Committee. My intention was that these committees, consisting of faculty, students, and administrators, would provide a vehicle by which the communities of color could share advice and guidance regarding the recruitment, retention, and graduation of minority students, as well as the scholarly success and satisfaction of minority faculty. I met with each committee monthly and held individual meetings with the committee chairs and was pleased with their generosity in contributing their time and expertise to this effort. They provided the university with invaluable guidance, input, feedback, and advice. They also identified and brought to our attention many issues and concerns specific to each community.

Within the first six months following my appointment, I was able to submit a report to the regents that outlined new recommendations on what the university could and should do to help remove barriers to the successful recruitment and retention of minority students and faculty. And I was proud to inform them of some recommendations that had already been implemented or were in the process of being implemented. I also recommended the establishment of a new annual process to handle the minority advisory committees' recommendations—a strong, inclusive process that included regular meetings with President Hasselmo to provide him with guidance and advice on addressing the university's diversity goals, followed by presidential instructions to the appropriate administrators to implement those goals. We would then receive advice from the administrators on the viability of those goals and timelines for implementation, and follow-up meetings with the committees would update them on the status of their recommendations and seek further feedback and advice.

Further, President Hasselmo directed that I submit an

annual report on the advisory committees' recommendations and how various administrative units implemented or acted on them. He also authorized support staff for each of the advisory committees to help facilitate this work. All of this enabled us to substantially enhance diversity on our campuses and to enhance the academic success of our minority students and faculty.

17

"RETIREMENT"

WHEN I HAD ACCEPTED THE POSITION and agreed to a three-year appointment, my initial goal was to see if I would be able to infuse diversity into the normal routines and functions of the operations and systems of this 141-year-old institution rather than simply introducing diversity into certain departments and activities. I knew it would be a difficult task, but I hoped that the changes I made as an associate vice president whose mission was diversity would continue to be implemented and the next administrator would have an environment in which to continue the diversity work. At the end of that three-year commitment, I was convinced that the recommendations I submitted to the president and the regents to meet that objective could be accomplished, but there would need to be an ongoing effort. With the help of my staff and the community, we had created a deeper awareness of the need for system-wide diversity. I felt I had successfully met my objective and that I had honored the purpose of the creation of the Office of Associate Vice President for Academic Affairs and Associate Provost with Special Responsibility for Minority Affairs.

I thought I might take a brief period of rest and relaxation after retirement, but looking back I truly do not remember stopping my instinctive behavior—justice and equality were still critical issues in our society. New things were developing in some of the organizations where I was serving as a board member when I retired. One board I continued to serve on was for the Minneapolis Institute of Arts (MIA). I had first become interested in the art museum shortly after Chuck and I moved to Minneapolis, and we took the girls there regularly. Back then the museum had a lending program where patrons could borrow artwork. We utilized the program one or two times, bringing art home to enjoy for the allotted time. I joined their board of trustees the year Patrice died, on the recommendation of my good friend Marvin Borman.

I believe I made a significant contribution to the organization's outreach efforts during my fifteen-year tenure as a trustee. I knew MIA was a place that Black people interested in the arts would want to visit and would also want to volunteer if opportunities were made available to them. I very much enjoyed working with Evan Maurer, who was the institute's director at the time. He was such a forward-thinking, civic-minded man, and he didn't doubt for a second that what I believed was true. He and our board fully supported my effort to develop a program that would support Black citizens who didn't have degrees in art history or the financial resources to become docents or active members of the institution. Evan was able to see that there are people in our community without those qualifications but with a deep love of art, who would very much enjoy serving as tour guides in the galleries. We created a program that provided twelve weeks of training, which included information about the organization, some of its holdings, specifically African and African American art, and art history. We launched the program in 1998 and called it Culture in Focus Tours.

The first exciting demonstration of our new tour guide opportunity was an exhibition of the work of Jacob Lawrence and his wife, Gwendolyn Knight—the first time the works of these outstanding artists were exhibited together. Evan and I were thrilled to see a much larger viewing audience from the minority community, and I remember the pride I felt when we brought the couple in for an artists' talk. The auditorium was packed, and the audience included a large number of Black people. It was also during my tenure that the museum canceled admission fees, making the museum accessible to all income levels. The Minneapolis Institute of Art remains accessible to people of color, and the free membership and admission policy is still in place.

My relationship to the university stayed strong as well. The year after I retired, the university established the Josie R. Johnson Award in recognition of my lifelong contributions to human rights and social justice, which guided my work with the civil rights movement, years of community service, and tenure at the University of Minnesota. The award honors University of Minnesota faculty, staff, and students who model the issues of human rights and social justice.

Several years later, the African American Leadership Forum established the Dr. Josie R. Johnson Leadership Academy, a yearlong leadership training program for young professionals and emerging leaders working for civil rights and social justice. Participants go on to work in business and philanthropy, government and politics, faith and religion, and community action.

For a time after retirement I remained on the board of the University of Minnesota Foundation, the organization that raises and manages funds for the university. Initially, I felt very free to share my thoughts about how the money could be used. But after a while I became concerned. In my associate vice president position, my staff and I brought Black students together at the beginning of every year and encouraged them to get involved in every aspect of university life—in the band, cheerleading, theater. I wanted them to know that the University of Minnesota was their university and that they should explore all that it had to offer. But I didn't see any images of Black students on the brochures and other publicity materials the foundation was using to recruit students. I brought up my concern at a board meeting, saying that Black prospective students needed to see themselves represented in materials we were using for recruitment efforts. I was disappointed when, during the conversation, I discovered that my concerns were not as uniformly understood as I thought. I was surprised that that observation had not been made by other members of the board and staff, and that the urgency for correcting the oversight did not seem to have exigency. The year after I resigned, I saw more inclusive images in the brochures.

Meanwhile, I joined the Women's Health Fund and served as president in 1999. Dr. June Lavalleur, a well-known obstetrician-gynecologist and researcher at University Hospital who had gone to medical school as a more mature student, was extremely engaged in getting the university to become more concerned about women's health issues. June was my doctor, and she and I always laugh when we talk about how she convinced me to join. I was in her office having my annual physical exam, and we were discussing the results of the examination when she asked me to join the board. Of course, I agreed. I was committed to bringing African American women on that board to help create a strong understanding of Black women's health issues. Bernadette Anderson, who was president of the Urban League Guild, accepted my invitation to join the Women's Health Fund board.

An exciting opportunity was presented to me during my first year of retirement: Reverend Alfred Babington-Johnson, president of the Stair Step Foundation, and his assistant, Menia Buckner, invited me and six other Black women to become members of a project sponsored by the reverend to travel to Ghana, in West Africa. Seven adult women would mentor seven high school girls on the trip, guiding them in life lessons as they all learned more about African culture and traditions. It was my first trip to Africa and it gave me many lasting memories. My dearest friend Katie McWatt was also one of the mentors. I laugh when I remember how difficult it was to encourage her to accept the invitation, as Katie was deathly afraid of flying. I was able to convince her that we would be safe, but what finally made her decision was our objective: she decided that serving our young girls was worth the trip.

It truly was a wonderful and educational experience. Menia was an excellent planner and organizer. She selected the hotel and the restaurants, as well the places we would visit, and she made sure that we had ample time together for meaningful discussions. Each mentor shared a hotel room with her mentee, and as a group we went on tours together during the day and met together in the evening to talk about what we had seen. We saw our people working together to clear roads and build homes in their communities. We visited markets and purchased things to bring home to our families.

We also visited what are known as the slave "castles." I do not understand why they are called castles, as they are really dungeons. I was shocked that you can still smell the stench of the suffering of our ancestors when we saw the small, small rooms they were forced to stay in, huddled together like they were in a can of sardines, exactly like pictures we have all seen. We couldn't hold back the tears when we saw the Door of No Return, through which they were led from those horrible dungeons to the slave ships.

A special opportunity for Katie and me was a visit to the W. E. B. Du Bois Research Center in Accra. As we entered and saw his desk and the materials he was working on at his desk, I imagined having a conversation with him. We appreciated the opportunity to see his work in his Ghana center. We took pictures and understood more clearly what he was doing in Ghana and why he had moved there.

178 Also, having read about the spiritual life of our ancestors, we were thrilled to visit a very mixed spiritual Sunday
church service that was unlike any I had ever seen. Held
in a large church that reminded me of a coliseum, it was a
remarkable gathering of people who practiced all kinds of
spiritual expressions. A minister spoke and a choir sang, and
then the congregants gathered into their own spiritual, tribal,
and cultural groups. Many small groups were speaking their
own languages and expressing their own spiritual rituals in
the same space. I was very moved to see the African cultural
traditions still alive and well. The night before we left Accra,
a tribal chief dressed in his traditional garments visited the
home of our host. He extended a traditional blessing, shared
the history of our Ghanaian ancestors, and then invited us
back "home."

Getting to know the young lady who was my mentee
and developing a personal and spiritual relationship have kept
us in touch. She went to college in Texas, then took a job
and moved to Texas. I remain in touch with her Minneapolis
family, her Texas baby boy, and her work history, and I see
her when she comes home to Minneapolis.

In 1995, a new state-of-the-art Harriet Tubman Women's
Shelter facility had opened in Minneapolis with a public
address. Going public was new for women's shelters at that
time because of very serious safety concerns—but the Tubman staff and board wanted to make the reality of violence
against women very visible, widely understood, and well
addressed by the whole community. The shelter was able to
do so because of extensive design and security measures that
made the new building completely secure. And three years
later a police precinct station opened across the street.

The new Harriet Tubman was very beautiful and very
large with an iron structure in the front created by local Black
artist Seitu Jones, which represented Harriet Tubman and

the struggle for freedom. In the new building we would be able to provide support and services ranging from immediate safety for women and children to long-term residencies. The facility made it possible to prepare women for lives without further abuse by offering human services, educational opportunities, and job training for gainful employment.

I was honored to be asked to play a major role in making the dreams for such an outstanding new facility a reality. It began in 1991, when I was invited to lunch by a good friend without any stated reason. I thought the invitation was nice but a little unusual: my friend Arthur T. Himmelman and I did not go out to lunch very often. We were enjoying our lunch and sharing our perspectives on many community issues as we usually did, but Arthur seemed to have something else on his mind. He told me later that he was as nervous as being in high school and asking a special girl to the prom.

I learned Arthur was nervous because, as he put it, he was on an incredibly important mission as the vice president of the Harriet Tubman board of directors and chair of its development committee. Arthur asked me to lunch to see if I would become the chair of the Harriet Tubman Campaign Committee to raise $6 million to design and construct its new facility. Arthur said he knew I was the best possible person to be campaign chair because I brought unquestioned integrity and credibility, long-term commitments to equity and justice, a lifetime of outstanding professional accomplishments, and a record of extraordinary service to those suffering from hardships in their lives. I was flattered to hear him tell me this and was interested in the idea of a new Tubman facility, but I could only respond by saying I would consider it over the next few days. Arthur was relieved I had not declined and waited, with some anxiety, until I contacted him with my answer. A conversation with Sharon Sayles Belton, who would later become the first woman and the first

Black mayor of Minneapolis, convinced me. She took me to the shelter on Oakland Avenue near Lake Street and told me it was established in 1976 as the third battered women's shelter in the country.

I agreed to chair the committee. However, I didn't wish to play this role without someone else I knew who could bring contacts, networks, and access to financial resources beyond my own, so I invited my friend Marvin Borman to co-chair with me and he graciously agreed. Marvin was highly respected as a brilliant lawyer, but even more so for the countless ways he worked tirelessly on behalf of people and communities in need. I knew then I could call Arthur and tell him Marvin and I would co-chair the committee.

The campaign for Tubman met its fund-raising goal and even exceeded it. While Marvin and I played important roles in making this possible, we also were members of a large team, which included other committee members, Tubman's board of directors, community members, and, most important, completely supported by Tubman's extremely capable executive director, Beverly Dusso, and her outstanding staff, which included Junauld Braddock-Presley who still serves as director of residential services.

Arthur told me about a moment prior to my involvement when Tubman board members were concerned about the difficulties in raising what was an unprecedented amount of money for a women's shelter at that time. As chair of the development committee, Arthur was asked about having a feasibility study done to see if the campaign goal was "realistic." Arthur told me he thought about the shelter choosing to call itself the Harriet Tubman Women's Shelter, thereby carrying forward her legacy of extraordinarily courageous and righteous actions to free men, women, and children from slavery at enormous personal risk to herself. Arthur then told the board members they did not need a feasibility study because they had chosen to name their services and support for women suffering from abuse in honor of Harriet Tubman. He believed they would succeed in the campaign because it was the right cause and was long overdue for more financial resources; because they were doing it in honor of one of the greatest heroic figures in American history; and because they greatly admired and deeply respect Harriet Tubman. Finally, they would succeed because they must do what she would do if she were living among us. And indeed we did succeed. The new facility was renamed the Harriet Tubman Center: the concept was that this center would follow the tradition of Harriet Tubman—in protecting mothers, children, and families, as the strong representative of this support of families.

One of the community members who served on our Tubman committee was a man named Clifton Johns, who was a member of the church located behind the Tubman, Redeemer Missionary Baptist Church. Cliff had become very concerned about the deterioration of the church building due to many years of poor maintenance and extreme moisture, which caused a leaking roof, mold, and other problems that he felt were a danger to the health of the church members. He wanted to restore the building to its original state. The restoration would be costly, so he asked me to join him in the effort. This was not an unusual request to me, as I knew Cliff from other community endeavors in addition to our work with the Tubman committee. Also, Tubman and Redeemer shared a parking lot. I felt that the Tubman Center and Redeemer Church had a very close relationship, and I was happy to work with him.

We were able to recruit a very enthusiastic group of people for our restoration committee, all of whom were also involved in the community. The committee met at Tubman and consisted of civil rights activists and people I knew from the community: Ford Bell of the James Ford Bell Foundation; Governor Mark Dayton's niece Megan Dayton;

Kathleen Fluegel and others whom I knew from the MIA board; Diane Neiman, who was the executive director of the Family Philanthropic Foundation; Penny and Mike Winton, other friends from the MIA; Clifton Johns; and the minister of the church, Reverend Alfred L. Harris.

They raised money, speaking on the church's behalf identifying its historical relationship to our city. The architecture firm we employed, MacDonald & Mack Architects, specializes in historic preservation and stewardship of existing structures of all ages, from prairie homesteads to streamlined modern landmarks. They saw great value in restoring the church and were able to locate historic documents and the church's history. We learned that it was built in 1910 as a Presbyterian church and was designed in the Prairie School style of architecture.

The restoration was completed in 2000 and became a very successful and important demonstration of historic preservation in the heart of the city; the project won the National Trust for Historic Preservation Honor Award. Part of the new design that I remember and that made the congregation happy was that the baptismal pool, which had always been in the lower level of the church, was redesigned so that it was brought up to the first floor, near where the minister spoke, giving it a broader viewing by the congregation during holy baptismal periods.

We had a wonderful, well-attended dedication. The community was invited and the congregation prepared refreshments. There were speakers who represented the work done on that beautiful structure, including the lovely, original wood and the opening of a huge set of folding doors that were more than fifteen feet high, which separated the sanctuary from the instructional part of the building where Bible studies and Sunday School were held. The newly restored building received great acclaim from all the people who had been a part of the project. The congregants who served on the committee were so proud—especially Cliff Johns, who had worked so hard on the project.

Another board that had a mission to reach out and serve the community was the Catholic Community Foundation of Minnesota. It is a branch of a worldwide philanthropic organization whose mission, in its own words, is "to provide funding for children's homes, hospitals, schools, universities, and social agencies throughout the world in direct response to Christ's teachings." Here in Minnesota, Catholic donors build on that sacred tradition. I served on the board for ten years, from 2001–2011, during the time that Archbishop Harry Joseph Flynn was chair and my own priest, Father Kevin McDonough, was also on the board. It was a wonderful opportunity to get to know Catholic individuals and to be of service to the communities of the Minneapolis–St. Paul archdiocese.

I served on the board in several capacities. I was on the executive committee, and I chaired the strategic planning committee and the grants committee, which received applications from groups that were requesting financial support from the foundation. While on that committee, I had a chance to visit various requesting groups and learned a lot about them. I enjoyed the opportunity to get to know the directors of those programs and the children who would benefit from the applied funds. One of the groups was our own WE WIN Institute, founded by Titilayo Bediako, the daughter of my dear friend Matthew Little. I derived a great sense of satisfaction knowing that we were actually able to fund one of the educational efforts in our city that addressed the needs of African American children.

In 1981, St. Peter Claver's school building had reopened and the church became rededicated to the mission of educating the children in the Rondo neighborhood. One day years later, in 2008, when I was seventy-eight, Father Kevin and I were having lunch, enjoying our usual conversations. The topic turned to the school, St. Peter Claver. Our principal, Teresa Mardenborough, was retiring. The most likely candidate to replace her was a teacher/coach already working in the school, but he needed time to complete his principal certification courses first and was scheduled to finish within a year. Father Kevin wanted to know if I would take the assignment for that year. I was willing to accept the terms—little compensation, twelve-hour days, seven days a week—starting immediately. I felt confident in my academic training, knowledge, years of experience in education, and faith in African American culture to do my job as principal.

I was blessed to be of service. I retired from that assignment in 2010. The school continues to model discipline, order, and academic excellence. I was able to engage the parents at a level that worked for them and our teachers. We encouraged civility among our students and support for all volunteers and after-school projects. Art, theater, geography, and politics at the appropriate grade level added to the knowledge of the upper grade students. There appeared to be satisfaction and success during that period. My service and experience at St. Peter Claver School was one of the most rewarding periods in my retiring years.

When Sharon Sayles Belton was first elected in 1994 as Minneapolis's first female and first Black mayor—in fact, the first Black mayor of any major city—Phyllis Goff organized a committee to sponsor a bust created in honor of her accomplishments. We worked for about a year but lost energy when it didn't appear that we would be successful. But Phyllis never lost interest. She reactivated the campaign in 2016 and brought together a diverse group of community people to serve as the Sharon Sayles Belton Bust Committee. She invited Reatha Clark King and me to co-chair the committee. We worked on the project for about a year and a half, and with the $100,000 we raised, we were able to contract Ed Dwight to create the bronze bust.

185

I knew Ed from Colorado when I contracted him to sculpt a bust of Lieutenant Governor George Brown, whom I had served as chief of staff. In his earlier career, Ed was an Air Force test pilot and was the first African American to be trained as an astronaut. Later, he studied art and became a sculptor, creating some thirty-five great works of celebratory African American art. His sculptures include international monuments to the Underground Railroad in Detroit and Canada; a memorial to Dr. Martin Luther King Jr. in Denver's City Park; a bust of George Washington Williams in the Ohio State Capitol in Columbus; the Black Patriots Memorial on the Mall in Washington, D.C.; the South Carolina Black History Memorial in Columbia; the Alex Haley–Kunta Kinte Memorial in Annapolis, Maryland; and the Quincy Jones Sculpture Park in Chicago. Some of his works are on permanent display at the Smithsonian Institute.

Ed created a beautiful bronze bust of Mayor Sayles Belton, unveiled at Minneapolis City Hall on May 16, 2017, to a crowd of three hundred people. It is one of only three busts that are displayed on the third floor of City Hall outside the offices of the Minneapolis City Council.

OUR ABIDING HOPE

AS I REVIEW my seven-plus decades of engagement in the struggle for justice, equality, and equal opportunity for African American people, I realize the struggle requires many different approaches. But what is consistent in this work is a determination to honor the historical struggle of our ancestors, and the belief in us as a people. We need to observe the world we live in, remember what has gone before us, assess results, and have understanding and empathy for all strategies. We should appreciate the efforts of our ancestors, whose love and care gave our children the confidence to be the best they can be. We need to understand the depth of the struggle, the history of the struggle, and the pain of the struggle. We need patience with those who need instant gratification, who have been deeply touched and wounded by supremacy and racism, who have only felt the pain of what has *not* worked. We must love and understand our brothers and sisters who have not been blessed with the love, security, and examples of belief in what's possible.

We need the energy to keep trying. Civil rights laws that began to take legal shape in the 1950s and 1960s were passed—but the teaching of white supremacy is stronger than laws. And so I learned from those around me that you don't stop; you keep on keeping on.

My generation participated in the process of appreciating and learning that "Black Is Beautiful," knowing that we were "Young, Gifted, and Black," listening and believing in words like "Hold On, Hope Is Coming." My generation understands why our children are impatient and continue to demonstrate against injustice. They will become ancestors themselves one day, and they too must believe that there is "hope in the struggle."

I never thought I would live long enough to see a Black president. I was seventy-eight years old when Barack Obama was elected to his first term as President of the United States in 2008.

As I reflect on my DFL and overall political involvement over the years, I realize how long and deep that history has remained. I have been involved in politics since I was fourteen years old, when I went door to door with my father in Houston to collect signatures to do away with the oppressive Poll Tax, which was implemented throughout the South to prevent Blacks from voting. I was twenty-one and living in Massachusetts with my husband in 1952 when I cast my first vote. President Harry Truman was elected that year. I have been involved in Minnesota politics since 1957 and have served in many capacities. I've been a precinct chair, a city and state delegate, a co-chair of the African American Caucus and the DFL party, along with many other roles. There is a brick that bears my name in front of the DFL headquarters in St. Paul, along with bricks with the names of others who have served the party over long periods of time. I remember celebrating the dedication of my brick with Jane Freeman, wife of former Governor Orville Freeman and mother of our current Hennepin County Attorney, Michael Freeman. My name had been suggested, among others, by the Black state legislators who were young activists when I became engaged in politics in Minnesota.

In 2006, I was on vacation with my family in St. Martin in the Caribbean when my son-in-law, Eugene Jones Duffy, received a call from Illinois Senator Barack Obama. The senator said he was being urged to run for President of the United States and asked for Gene's financial support if he decided to accept the challenge. At that time, I didn't believe America was ready to elect a Black person to represent the nation on the world stage. I advised Gene that the election would never happen and financial support would not help Senator Obama's campaign, but he ignored my advice and agreed to support the senator. He worked very hard, raised lots of money, sponsored, and cosponsored many events in Atlanta, where he and my daughter Norrene reside, and across the nation.

Even though I held a deep feeling that this country was not ready for Barack Obama, I decided to work hard for him as well. Initially, I made phone calls, registered voters, spoke on his behalf whenever and wherever I could, and contributed financially as often as my resources would allow. As I became more involved in the campaign, I wanted to become a delegate to the 2008 Democratic National Convention in Denver. That a Black man, a descendant of African ancestors, a people despised by the laws, teachings, and behaviors of a nation, would be selected to represent America in my lifetime seemed unbelievable. And the thought that I could be engaged in the process of selecting him as a nominee was beyond a dream come true.

The path to the convention as a delegate required advice and guidance. There is an established and respected process for becoming a delegate to the national convention, a process that includes candidates from the congressional and state districts, representatives from the elected congressional members, and Democratic National Committee members. During my early affiliation, the Party added gender and race to the selection of delegates. By this time, gender was the main criterion added to the selection process, and Affirmative Action

language used for the process was changed from racial composition of the state to include both racial and gender balance
so that there would be an equal number of male and female
delegates as well as delegates from different racial groups.

I was blessed to know RoseAnn Zimbro, the outreach
director for the Minnesota DFL. She was an excellent trainer,
with serious attention to detail regarding the processes
required to earn the honor of being elected as a national delegate. RoseAnn maintained that half of the battle to becoming a delegate is knowing and following the rules for delegate
selection. I had been a delegate in our city and state conven-
tions, but this was different—I was eager to attend the convention of a lifetime.

The Democratic National Convention has a system where
unpledged delegates known as superdelegates are seated auto-
matically and can choose for themselves who they wish to
support for a presidential nomination. Minnesota has two
delegates, one male and one female. My name was placed in
nomination at the state convention and I was voted to be one
of the two superdelegates from Minnesota. I was going to the
August 27 National Convention in Denver.

It was a great feeling being back in Denver for a brief
while, even though we were busy, and I was able to see a
lot of my old political friends. It was also pleasing to see that
the delegation of people who attended the convention conducted a food drive—we must have packaged hundreds of
food boxes to share with the community of Denver.

A motion to nominate Barack Obama as the Democratic
nominee by acclamation was presented by Hillary Clinton
and was unanimously accepted. Barack Hussein Obama was
now the official candidate for President of the United States
of America. This gracious action improved my attitude about
her, and I was happy to have an opportunity to speak with her
and former President Clinton while I was there. I also had a
chance to meet future Senator Kamala Harris from California.

Her niece and my granddaughter Josie Helen are very good friends, and they were both at the convention as well. Another wonderful thing that occurred was that Byron Pitts, who was at CBS at the time, interviewed me to get my perspective on the support of Obama and what my hopes were and what I thought his election would mean for our efforts in the struggle. I was very impressed with his interview.

Amazingly, the day our first African American presidential nominee gave his acceptance speech, August 28, 2008, was the forty-fifth anniversary of the day the Reverend Martin Luther King Jr. delivered his iconic "I Have a Dream" speech at the March on Washington—a speech I also witnessed. All of the Black delegates in the room were so proud, and none of us oldsters could believe we were seeing this happen after all those years of not believing it was even a possibility. It was a happy, cheerful moment, and yet there wasn't a dry eye in the room.

President Barack Obama was sworn into office as the forty-fourth president on January 20, 2009. It was a historic moment in American history, a dream deferred for so long. I was blessed to see and to visit with President Obama on several occasions, and to visit with the First Lady. And to think those blessings began with a phone call a young senator from Illinois made to my son-in-law in 2006.

Early in President Obama's first term, Representative Keith Ellison invited me and his wife, Kim, and their daughter to attend First Lady Michelle Robinson Obama's first public event in Washington, D.C., a luncheon she sponsored to say thank you to women campaigners and others. Rather than gifting us with things that wouldn't last such as flowers, Mrs. Obama gave each of her guests a pair of sandals—something that would be comfortable, lasting, and sustainable for us. I met Michelle Obama on two other occasions during the campaigns in 2008 and again in 2011.

Representative Ellison also invited me to the president's

first State of the Union speech. I was sitting in the balcony of the House of Representatives chamber listening proudly and intently. I will never forget the moment when the president began to speak about health care. Suddenly, Republican Representative Joe Wilson of South Carolina yelled, "You lie." I saw the president pause for a moment and look in Representative Wilson's direction. I couldn't believe what I had heard. The President of the United States of America was being publicly disrespected by an elected U.S. Representative.

The shock of that experience should have prepared us for what was to become a pattern of behavior. Members of the Republican Congress announced immediately after his election that they would not support his office or his legislation and would oppose his leadership in every way possible. They did not make these statements behind closed doors: they publicly made their position clear and followed up at every possible opportunity. Yet in spite of their declarations, under President Obama America was in the most envied position in the world, and he was elected to a second term.

The election of Donald John Trump defied everything experts predicted and was a blow to the Black community. My family, friends, and colleagues were devastated. Unfortunately, it was not a shocking surprise to me. I was disappointed but I really was not surprised. Over time, my observation has been that the degree of hatred that those who enslaved our ancestors perpetrated toward Black people is deeply etched into the psyche of America. The justification that was given for enslaving our ancestors and the treatment and the teaching of inferiority of Black people have created a lasting problem. Donald Trump was able to preach supremacy of white people and to invoke insecurity by tapping into the fears taught about Black people during slavery. He was able to offer those facing economic hardship a target for their anger and frustration. The multitudes who attended his public rallies and other gatherings suggested to me that he was delivering a message that was being heard and approved by a large number of Americans. His rhetoric, style, and lies were drawing very large crowds. It was becoming pretty clear that there were more people approving of his style and supporting his campaign strategy than we realized.

Trump's belief in white supremacy shouldn't have been a surprise to any of us. He has a long and documented history of showing bias in both his business and political life dating as far back as the 1960s. In fact, much of what he said during his campaign was reminiscent of hateful things I heard throughout the civil rights struggle. And I remembered that he was the leader of the "birther" movement, a movement that insisted that Barack Hussein Obama was born in Kenya and that therefore he was not qualified to be the President of the United States of America.

What was shocking and troubling to me was that no matter what he said or did, Trump was able to garner widespread support, even from those whom he publicly disdained. He was cruel and mean spirited, and a bully to other candidates. He was vulgar in his language and description of relations with and expressions toward women and consistently modeled sexist beliefs, and yet white women voted for him in large numbers. He openly mocked people with disabilities and disrespected nonwhite families whose children had died and earned medals for their service to our country. He, without shame, showed himself to be self-absorbed—and he lied over and over again. Even individuals who were respected leaders with authority and power in their religious faith communities were willing to overlook his lack of spiritual knowledge and his lack of respect for those who had spiritual beliefs.

Mr. Trump demonstrated repeatedly that he did not know American history or the language of the Constitution of the United States of America, and that he had little knowledge of world history or customs. He seemed not to care, nor was he interested in learning. And I began to believe that his followers did not care either. In fact, it seemed that the less he knew, the larger his following. As I sat watching on November 4, 2016, the vote count for Donald Trump became an issue. And as I answered phone calls from family and friends who were also watching his results climb, many became deeply afraid and prayed that there would be a different result.

My family and friends were in disbelief when it was announced that Donald J. Trump had been elected President of the United States of America.

My eldest granddaughter, Lauren Noelle Thomas Araujo, and I talked for more than an hour the morning the election results were confirmed. Lauren tearfully expressed her fears about the future her two little girls might have to face. She was afraid that her children may have to fight during their lifetime what their great-grandmother had fought during her lifetime. She asked, "When will we be free?"

I understood her fears. I was the third generation out of slavery and was still fighting for justice. I tried to give her hope and encouragement. I told her that hope is what gives us a sense of movement and energy. Hope moves us to remember the struggle of our ancestors. Hope reminds us to "keep on keeping on," as my father used to say. Hope forces us to do the next thing in our struggle, to try another approach in our collective work. Our ancestors showed us how to love each other, take care of our children, keep our spiritual faith, and know that "this too shall pass." I said that by the time my great-grandchildren, Lauren Noelle's daughters, Lucy Josephine and Ella May, and granddaughter Josie Helen's son, Niko, are assuming their place in the world, they will be ready for whatever is there for them to continue. We will outlast Trump. I must admit, though, for a moment

I had to call on the ancestors to remind me who I am and whose shoes I stepped into many years ago.

I was with my daughter Norrene and her family in Atlanta when Trump took his oath of office. My children Josie Irene, Norrene Elaine, and my son-in-law Eugene, who was so instrumental in getting Obama elected, were shocked that America would elect a person such as Trump had demonstrated himself to be. I believe they thought that we as a nation were further along than I thought we were. And I believe that African Americans were eager to hold on to the hope, direction, honesty, and spirituality that Obama evoked. But our main pride was in how he had pulled America out of the depths of a financial crisis and in the process provided hope to the country and to the people who were suffering from the recession when he took office in 2008. This nation was on the edge of an economic disaster and Obama returned America to financial health. It was shocking to me to realize that supremacy and the Trump philosophy, as spoken and demonstrated, could supersede all that President Obama had accomplished without the support of members of Congress—a Congress that had promised on the night of his first State of the Union address to not support him or his goals for America. The fact that America was willing to sacrifice all of that was a real surprise. My children were as surprised and disappointed as I was. I remember the night we got the results my daughter Josie said, "Mother, we as a people have withstood so much throughout our history. We will survive this as well."

Since his election, Donald Trump has defined his presidency in his own way. He has borrowed strategies from past presidents, for example, Nixon and Reagan, that fit his definition of his presidency. And in so doing, he has created a world of confusion. He is clearly and proudly not organizing his administration on a model of tradition and history. His method of governing does not fit anything scholars of politics or writers of political history have ever seen or experienced. Instead, he gives respect and value to his determination to change the system and to his ignorance of history, tradition, and protocol. His intent to disrupt the system has influenced his selection of members of his cabinet, and he appoints those who do not trust the government he is now managing. He has appointed individuals who seem to lack the skills, knowledge, or commitment to America. Trump's philosophy seems to be to divide and conquer. He seems to enjoy creating confusion. President Obama did not have enough support from Congress to get his legislation passed into laws and had to use executive orders to make a difference during his two terms in office. Trump makes no secret that his mission to "make American great again" means to undo everything Obama did. Unfortunately, he has the authority to do so.

I agree with my daughter Josie. Indeed, we have withstood and survived, as a people, the history of the denial of much of our history—and will survive this as well. In the meantime, my children and grandchildren are addressing their fears and responses in different ways: from managing their co-workers with justice and fairness, to writing legal blogs on topics of justice and fairness, to studying and understanding Black culture through the arts. By focusing on who we are and what we have contributed and passing their knowledge on, they are carrying on our family tradition of being ambassadors of our culture and history.

As I review my understanding of the election of Mr. Trump and reflect on the fears of my grandchildren, I appreciate more and more clearly the impulse of their generation to ask why we still struggle for justice and equality. My continued struggle comes from my belief in the history and experience of African American people and our determination to survive for our children. I believe the protection and love of community and what we want for our children are factors

196

in how we have gotten beyond any hopeless moment in our history. Somehow, we have always been able to pass that strength on to the next generation. We have experienced every type of abuse, brutal government leadership, and denial of human and civil rights. We have seen and survived other Trumps. We have modeled creativity, intelligence, determination, and skill. I do not believe the method Trump is modeling as American democracy will last. We are survivors. We will be here when the Mr. Trumps of the world are exposed and out of power. We will save our children and will continue in the tradition of our ancestors. We will survive, we will live, and we will have hope.

Acknowledgments

I cannot imagine taking this life journey or persisting in this work without the support and companionship of my family and friends. Throughout the process of writing this book, I have felt their spirits. I have been inspired by their commitments to our struggle and to our community, and I have remembered our collective obligation to our ancestors and children.

My daughters, Josie Johnson Thomas and Norrene Johnson Duffy, have been right here at my hip with love and support in every way that I could expect (even after the many late dinners of their childhood). I rely on their honest counsel and lean on their understanding. They make me feel useful and worthy of anything that I receive. That my daughters have encouraged their own children—my granddaughters, Lauren Noelle, Josie Helen, and Rosa Patrice—to live their lives in commitment to community gives me deep satisfaction. Part of my hope for this book is that my grandchildren and my three great-grandchildren will not have to fight against the humiliation, pain, and lack of fulfillment that have been the struggle of my generation, and that Black children in all future generations experience the dignity and respect due every human being.

I am happy that my daughter Norrene Elaine married

Eugene Jones Duffy. Eugene comes from a family of pioneers in the struggle for freedom and justice; his parents, Frank and Helen, taught him and his siblings to be proud of their ancestry and to be workers for justice. The Duffys have become my other family and helped to make the past thirty-plus years very rewarding and fulfilling. Frank and Helen's children and grandchildren have been a source of immense joy and an extraordinary blessing. Crowned Grandma Josie, I have been embraced by generations and loved with reverence, affection, and tenderness. Our gatherings renew my spirit and cause me to celebrate the special nature of family in our community and provoke me to count my blessings.

Mahmoud El-Kati, my dearest friend and brother, has been my thought-partner and teacher in our struggle for justice and equality for more than fifty years. In our African tradition and culture, Mahmoud and his wife, TiTi, gave me the gift of being the godmother of their daughter Kamali and celebrated this gift in a community naming ceremony. His example in writing about and studying the history of Black people, his commitment to addressing issues of justice with adults and young people, and his enthusiasm and support have given me the courage to write this book. His love, respect, and belief in me have motivated me to tell this story of struggle and hope.

I will always feel lucky and blessed to have had Matthew Little, Katie McWatt, and Max Fallek in my life. The deaths of my dear friends—my sister Katie in 2009 and Matt in 2016—brought me pain and loneliness that I still feel today. Katie modeled the struggle and capacity of Black women through her political activities, her counsel to youth, and her example of courage to her family. Matt never forgot the legal and political issues of our time even as he tirelessly continued the mission of the NAACP. Max Fallek has been and continues to be a dear friend and companion over a lifetime of work, especially at the Urban League, The Way, and the March on Washington.

In 1948, when I was a sophomore at Fisk University, we had the privilege of hearing many lectures about the civil rights movement, the second Reconstruction, and Blacks who served in the U.S. Congress from 1929 and beyond. We also knew the history of our Black national anthem, "Lift Every Voice and Sing," composed by James Weldon Johnson who taught at Fisk, my alma mater.

In addition to the many Black luminaries who taught and lectured at Fisk, we also learned about Hubert H. Humphrey, who as mayor of Minneapolis and a member of the Platform Committee for that year's National Democratic Convention held in Philadelphia had delivered a powerful address in support of civil rights, which established Minnesota as a state where racial equality was taken seriously, causing thirty-five delegates from Mississippi and Alabama to walk out of the convention. To hear a national leader reflect what Black leaders had been preaching throughout the history of Black people in America was an impressive and historical moment. Refreshing, hopeful, profound.

Humphrey had not yet become the thirty-eighth Vice President of the United States when Charles and I moved to Minneapolis in 1956. At that time, he was serving as a U.S. senator from Minnesota. I learned much more of his history when I served as assistant to Minneapolis mayor Art Naftalin when I was on leave from the Urban League in the 1960s. Art had worked as Humphrey's assistant when he was a senator and, like Humphrey, was deeply involved in civil rights issues. The development of the Minneapolis Human Rights Department was modeled after the department created by Hubert Humphrey when he was our mayor. I received the Hubert H. Humphrey Public Leadership Award in 2007 from the University of Minnesota and the Hubert H. Humphrey award for Dedication and Leadership to the Minnesota DFL Party on March 15, 2008. I have served and participated in many Humphrey School of Public Affairs events, speaking to international student classes and gatherings at public community affairs. I have felt deeply honored to be associated with the history of Hubert H. Humphrey.

I was also blessed to know Norman Sherman, a very important mentee of Vice President Humphrey, and to read his book *From Nowhere to Somewhere,* which gives a great understanding of the influence Humphrey had on the civil rights efforts in both Minnesota and the nation.

My proudest honor with regard to the vice president came when I was invited to speak at the unveiling of the Hubert H. Humphrey Memorial on the State Capitol Grounds on August 4, 2012. President Bill Clinton, Senator Al Franken, Arne Carlson, and Senator Amy Klobuchar were also on the program.

Former Republican governor and lifelong friend Elmer Andersen contributed to my belief that politicians can make a difference when they are committed to the issues of justice and equality. Another lifelong friend, former mayor Art Naftalin, was a champion for justice throughout our many years of community service. My colleague in work for fair housing in Minnesota, Zetta Feder, was a close personal friend. Our families shared many holidays and enjoyed many leisure events and activities together. I will always deeply appreciate her commitment to legislative success.

I will always feel blessed to have been introduced to Paul Wellstone and his wife, Sheila, when I returned to Minnesota. From that moment on, he became a close friend and adviser, and I felt very privileged to be among those he invited to be engaged in his thought process. I was devastated at the news of his death. In my judgment, he was a voice of justice, fairness, courage, and love of the people. Sheila was his companion, his supporter, and his strength. They will always have a special place in my belief in the struggle for justice.

Several dear friends and fellow educators have been important to my work. Gisela Konopka was an inspirational educator and champion for troubled children. Gisa and I team-taught an experimental course in the mid-1960s at the University of Minnesota on racism and troubled African American youth. She always had her calendar and small pencil ready to make another appointment to discuss strategies for saving children who needed their voices heard. Sara Roberson and I have known each other and been friends since 1957; we carpooled our children to the University of Minnesota early childhood and elementary school program. Sara became an elementary school teacher in the Minneapolis public schools and courageously introduced the history of Native Americans to public school students in and beyond Minnesota. Barbara Shin and Rosilyn Carroll taught public school teachers methods and curricula for educating children of diverse backgrounds. I want to recognize singer and songwriter Larry Long for his efforts celebrating everyday heroes and elders—especially his work with the students at Emerson Immersion School and their program honoring me and sharing the values of justice and advice from our ancestors transferring across generations.

I have known Gary Cunningham since he was a University of Minnesota student, and I have always felt free and safe to share my ideas about community issues with him. I am so appreciative of his contributions to the establishment of the Leland–Johnson Common Vision Program and for his support and savvy insights in our discussions of the issues of justice and equality for our community.

Vernon H. Wilson was a trustee and anchor at St. Peter Claver. He had keys to the church and deposited the Sunday collections. He was an usher and kept record of candles and sacrament supplies. Vernon was the trusted, dependable, and deeply spiritual leader in the church. He had been a member for many years and worked as a chemist at 3M Corporation. I got to know Vernon in 2005, and we have been friends ever since. I know his children and assisted in the wedding of his son. As Vernon's health declines, I am blessed to be the person here to serve him and thank him for all he has done for me in the years we have known each other. I feel like a member of his family.

As I have gotten older, I rely on the support of many people for the business of living. The love, care, and technical assistance of Rhonda Franklin have been special blessings in the many years we have known each other. I have depended on Rhonda in so many ways, and she never tires of my asking for help—from her trust in me and honoring me as the godmother of her only child to my late-hours, long-distance calls to ask, "What do I do? What is wrong with this computer?" she has been there for me. The loving care, the transportation, the regular assurance that I have food, and the daily assurance that I am okay come from my dear Martha Arradondo. My longtime friend Tyrone Tyrell is always available to come to my aid, acknowledge my special needs, and assure me nothing is too much to ask. Frank Perkins regularly checks in on my needs and offers untiring assistance of any type. Bill and Frances Woodson are always there for me, and Julius Dixon provides a reminder of the care we, as a people, learned from our ancestors—the care of our elders.

Writing this book has not been an easy task for me, and it would not have happened without the help and contributions of a village of people.

Bill Davis, Anura and Rekhet Si-Asar, and Ellen Benavides were clear and convincing in articulating the necessity of this book and its value for young people. Kapria White, the granddaughter of Luther and Evelyn Prince, whom we knew from MIT and later Honeywell, became like one of my children: she is very close to me and looks to me as a grandmother, and I love her as a granddaughter. RoseAnn Zimbro, Harry "Spike" Moss, Leland Carriger, Makeda Zulu-Gillespie, and many others supplemented my memory by providing details of experiences and events discussed in this book. Maryama Dahir, Rekhet Si-Asar, Trisha Anderson, Cecily Marcus, Lisa Vecoli, and the exceedingly competent staff at the Givens Collection of African American Literature at the University of Minnesota and the University of Minnesota Archives helped to organize the many boxes of papers that were the reference materials for the writing of this book. Hadiya Shire and Aria Gilliam supported our writing with valuable transcription services. I deeply appreciate former mayor Sharon Sayles Belton, Dr. John Wright, Dr. Samuel Myers Jr., Kathleen O'Brien, Dr. Carol McGee Johnson, and Mahmoud El-Kati, who shared their insights through interviews that framed and affirmed the rationale for telling my story.

I feel blessed to publish with the University of Minnesota Press and in particular to work with Erik Anderson. Erik's deep listening, patience, careful editorial attention, and guidance have been essential for preparing and sharing my story with the community. I am also very grateful to Louisa Castner, who understood my story and helped my team and me in the editing of this book. Thank you.

Last but not least, this book would not have happened without the diligent and loving toil of Arleta Little and Carolyn Holbrook. Throughout our work and many discussions, our team has shared a commitment to preserving African American culture, sharing African American stories, and advancing justice for African American people. Over the journey of this book, I have felt joy and blessing that these women chose to exercise their talents in documenting my story. Arleta has been my thought-partner, trusted adviser, support, and confidant from the beginning of this eight-year project. She skillfully outlined the orienting framework and values that have been our guide over many years and ultimately assisted in the writing of the book. I also relied on her to manage the project's financial and human resources. As a writer, Carolyn remained steadfastly committed (even through hundreds of pages, drafts, and transcripts) to capturing and articulating my thoughts in a coherent and comprehensive way. With careful observation and determined effort over many hours, we bridged generational differences and had a meeting of the minds. Carolyn's diligent research and sensitivity to detail have indelibly enriched the telling of my story.

Only limitations in space have prevented me from specifically mentioning the many other members of my community who generously contributed to the completion of this work. To all, I offer my gratitude for your many gifts and for your confidence in the enduring culture of our people.

204

The University of Minnesota Press gratefully acknowledges the generous assistance provided for the publication of this book from the following individuals.

Anonymous
Dr. Ford Watson Bell
Carol and Alan Bensman
Harry C. Boyte
Robert H. Bruininks and Susan A. Hagstrum
Philip C. Brunelle
Ellis F. Bullock Jr.
Burton D. Cohen
Richard A. Copeland
Gary Cunningham
Barbara Greenwald Davis
Lillian and Max Fallek
Barbara L. Forster
David C. Higgs
Sally E. Howard
Senator Amy J. Klobuchar
Benjamin Mchie
Dick P. Moe
Walter F. Mondale
Lee Sheehy and Cathy Lawrence
Josie Thomas
Penny Rand Winton

Index

Born in 1930 in San Antonio, Texas, JOSIE R. JOHNSON has been an educator, activist, and public servant for more than seven decades. Along with her work for the Urban League and the University of Minnesota, she served as office manager, campaign manager, and chief of staff for multiple political campaigns and public officials and has been co-chair of the African American DFL Caucus in Minnesota. She holds degrees in sociology, education, and education administration. She lives in Minneapolis and continues to serve her community, advocating for equal rights and social justice.

CAROLYN HOLBROOK is a writer, educator, and founder of More Than a Single Story, a program of public conversations with writers of color. She teaches creative writing at Hamline University and is author of *Ordinary People, Extraordinary Journeys,* which profiles twenty nonprofit leaders in Minnesota. In 2010 she received the Kay Sexton Award from the Friends of the St. Paul Public Library.

ARLETA LITTLE is director of artist fellowships for the McKnight Foundation. Prior to working in philanthropy, she was executive director of the Givens Foundation for African American Literature. Her writing was most recently published in *Blues Vision: African American Writing from Minnesota.*